THREE PLAYS

Other Plays by George Shiels

TWO IRISH PLAYS
THE PASSING DAY AND THE JAILBIRD
THE RUGGED PATH AND THE SUMMIT

THREE PLAYS

PROFESSOR TIM
PAUL TWYNING
THE NEW GOSSOON

BY

GEORGE SHIELS

LONDON
MACMILLAN & CO. LTD
1945

Professor Tim and *Paul Twyning* were first published in 1927,
The New Gossoon in 1936

Reissued in one volume, 1945

Amateur Societies desiring to perform these plays must first
obtain a permit from the author or his agent

PRINTED IN GREAT BRITAIN
BY R. & R. CLARK, LIMITED, EDINBURGH

CONTENTS

PROFESSOR TIM

A Comedy in Three Acts

Professor Tim was first produced at the Abbey Theatre, Dublin, on September 14, 1925, with the following cast:

JOHN SCALLY, *a Farmer*	Eric Gorman
MRS. SCALLY, *his Wife*	Sara Allgood
PEGGY SCALLY, *their Daughter* . . .	Eileen Crowe
PROFESSOR TIM, *Mrs. Scally's Brother* . .	F. J. McCormick
JAMES KILROY, *a Rural Councillor* . . .	Peter Nolan
MRS. KILROY, *his Wife*	Christine Hayden
JOSEPH KILROY, *their Son*	Barry FitzGerald
HUGH O'CAHAN, *a Sporting Farmer* . .	P. J. Carolan
PADDY KINNEY, *his Groom*	Arthur Shields
MOLL FLANAGAN, *his Housekeeper* . . .	Maureen Delany
MR. ALLISON, *an Auctioneer*	J. Stephenson

ACTS I and III.—John Scally's kitchen.
ACT II.—O'Cahan's dining-room.

The play was produced by Michael J. Dolan.

ACT I

JOHN SCALLY'S *kitchen: large and comfortably furnished, with a large table and a small one, a number of chairs, an old lounge, and a cupboard with glass door above and wooden doors below. The upper part is packed with china, the under part with linen, etc.*

At the back are two windows and a half-glass door leading to the farmyard. Another door, left, communicates with the hall. Fireplace on the right.

It is a July morning with a strong sun shining on the back windows.

PEGGY, *an attractive girl of about twenty-six, is doing laundry-work at the table.*

PEGGY [*after a hasty glance at the windows she takes some pieces of jewellery from her pocket and puts them on a piece of paper. She slips on and off a ring, then puts it with the rest and ties the parcel*]. I wish this day was finished!

HUGH O'CAHAN *enters on tiptoe, left. He is twenty-five, dressed in old riding-breeches and check jacket, and has a hunting-crop in his hand. He wears neither a collar nor tie.*

O'CAHAN. I was listening, Peggy, to make sure you were alone, and heard you sighing.

PEGGY. Hugh! how did you get in?

O'CAHAN. By the old route, dear; the parlour window.

PEGGY. I suppose you knocked down the plant.

O'CAHAN. You and that plant, Peggy! I've only

S   3

touched it once in four years, and that night there
was an eclipse of the moon.

PEGGY. Are you riding?

O'CAHAN. No, worse luck. For the first morning
in my life I've no horse to ride. Just this whip left.
. . . I wonder how long it is since the O'Cahans
had no horse? How long since the stables at Rush
Hill were last empty? It must be a good few
hundred years.

PEGGY. You'd a horse yesterday.

O'CAHAN. Yes, Havoc. But he, poor thing, was
removed last night. He went away as sad as a
Christian. Which left me without a four-footed
animal, except the cat. I'm a pretty handy fellow,
Peggy, but I can't ride a cat.

PEGGY. Did anyone see you coming in?

O'CAHAN. Not a soul. Your mother's feeding
young calves in the paddock, your father's driving
out a long string of cows, and hours ago I saw your
brothers and sisters going down the bog-road to
work. They were singing like birds.

PEGGY. They've gone over to the other farm to
make hay.

O'CAHAN. Their industry is shocking.

PEGGY. Well, Hugh, nobody can say that about
you.

O'CAHAN. Eh? Are you set on giving me a final
lecture? A few nice proverbs on the day I'm to be
auctioned out would improve me. . . .

PEGGY. I've no intention of lecturing. A ruined
man needs no lecture. He's a lecture to look at.

O'CAHAN. A ruined man at twenty-five! Talk
sense, Peggy. You can't ruin a man at that age —
not if you cut him in two. I've had my fling,

Peggy; it's all over but the auction, and I don't regret it.

PEGGY. I'm glad you've no regrets. [*Takes out packet.*] I've your ring and presents here: I want to return them.

O'CAHAN. Ah! I hadn't thought of this. But Lady Fate doesn't do her work slipshod; she keeps the big hammer for the last blow. . . . But you might keep those things, Peggy — just to spite the hag.

PEGGY. Impossible. You must take them back. They're valuable, and you may need the money.

O'CAHAN. Yes, I'm sure to need money. I need some now. [*Takes the packet and looks round.*] Have you no fire here?

PEGGY. No, we let it go out after breakfast.

O'CAHAN. And where, if it's a fair question, do you heat your irons?

PEGGY. There's a fire over in the old kitchen.

O'CAHAN [*going*]. Well, I'll add some fuel to it. . . .

PEGGY [*stops him*]. Hugh, you mustn't go out there. Mother would see you. Don't be foolish. . . .

O'CAHAN [*comes back*]. Nothing foolish about me, Peggy. I've always been famous for my wisdom. [*Hefting packet*] This was a prudent investment . . . three hundred pounds. Do you remember the day I made the purchase?

PEGGY. No.

O'CAHAN. You mean yes. I remember it too. I'd sold a mare and foal for a thousand guineas. I thought you and I were going to marry and I rushed off and bought these family jewels. . . . Well, it was all a mistake.

PEGGY. Stop, Hugh, please. I remember it only too well.

O'CAHAN. And this is the end of the story. I somehow can't believe it. Can you?

PEGGY. We've both got to believe it. It's the only way to end it: you're free and so am I.

O'CAHAN. Well, I must say you've cut it down fine. You've left it to within an hour of the auction to deliver the knock-out.

PEGGY. I left it as long as I could, Hugh — till there wasn't a gleam of hope anywhere.

O'CAHAN. The auction wasn't enough for one day — it just needed this to finish it. . . . Here, Peggy, take these things back.

PEGGY. I can't, Hugh. And I always told you it was folly putting so much money in presents. Something at half a crown would have done just as well.

O'CAHAN. Perhaps. But I didn't want a half-crown sweetheart, nor a half-crown wife. A woman at that price is usually very dear in the end. [*Offers packet*] Here, Peggy: take them and keep them. They'll remind you of a very foolish fellow.

PEGGY. I can't, Hugh.

O'CAHAN. You mean you won't?

PEGGY. I won't.

O'CAHAN. Then, to blazes with that! [*Flings it across the kitchen.*] And with every romantic thing on this earth!

PEGGY [*picks it up*]. I see now what you want. You want to make trouble. . . .

O'CAHAN. Trouble — who for?

PEGGY. For me . . . if mother comes in. Here, put this in your pocket. You can throw it into the river.

o'CAHAN. You live as near the river as I do. Drown them yourself. Or make jam of them. . . .

PEGGY. You needn't storm. I'll find some means of returning them. [*Puts them in her pocket.*]

o'CAHAN. I'll tell you how to dispose of them: hang them on Joseph Kilroy. They'll improve the cow's face of him.

PEGGY [*wincing*]. What do you mean, Hugh?

o'CAHAN. Ah, you must think Hugh's mighty green. It's a wonder the goats don't mistake me for brussels sprouts.

PEGGY. You can be very nasty.

o'CAHAN. Never without reason. You've kept Joseph Kilroy tied to your apron-strings to see how things would pan out at Rush Hill. He walks after you like a sheep. I saw you together last night. Is that nasty?

PEGGY. Hugh, you never look at my side of it at all. I've three sisters and three brothers, all single. That's too many single people in one house.

o'CAHAN. Well, why don't they all get married?

PEGGY. They were waiting for me to break the ice, and I was waiting for — well, I don't want to hurt you.

o'CAHAN. You're very considerate. . . . Didn't I want to marry you two years ago? And who objected?

PEGGY. Everybody objected. They saw the pace you were going and knew how it would end. Everybody could see that but yourself.

o'CAHAN. You were all great prophets! The Wise Men of the East weren't a patch on you. But I must say you played the waiting game not badly.

When I got a good price for a colt your mother smiled like a basketful of cats, and when I buried one she frowned like a gargoyle.

PEGGY. Whether you got a good price for a colt or buried it made no difference to me. You know that very well, but in your ugly mood you won't admit it.

O'CAHAN. Well, it doesn't matter a pin now anyway. The auction's at eleven o'clock. This morning I was sorry, but now I'm glad it's so near. Sale or no sale, I'm clearing out to-night.

PEGGY. Do you mind telling me where you're going?

O'CAHAN. I wouldn't mind telling you if I knew myself. But I've no plans. I may go to South America or Australia: some place where the horse isn't doomed for another generation.

PEGGY. You and the horse!

O'CAHAN. Yes, me and the horse! You'll have no trouble on that score with Joseph Kilroy. He couldn't lead a horse to the forge.

PEGGY. All the better for himself.

O'CAHAN. As I said, I can go where I please, and never look back. No home ties. I'm that rare bird you often hear of in Ireland but seldom see — the last man of his race.

PEGGY. Well, Hugh, mother'll be in soon. I must say good-bye.

O'CAHAN. Is that the whole farewell?

PEGGY. What's the good of anything more?

O'CAHAN. Not a bit. [*Buttoning his jacket*] I apologise, Peggy, for having crossed your path.

PEGGY. And I for crossing yours.

O'CAHAN. You crossed mine at a critical time.

I was twenty and riding straight for the cliff. If you'd followed up your success and married me, there'd be no auction to-day.

PEGGY. If!

O'CAHAN. Why draw my attention to it? " If " is an old friend of mine. My whole life has been dotted with " ifs ". If an old woman hadn't put out her washing on a certain day, I wouldn't have been an orphan at three years old. If a gust of wind hadn't blown her washing across the road, my father's horse would have trotted on home. . . .

PEGGY. Stop, Hugh. I know the rest.

O'CAHAN. If they'd kept the news from mother for three days she might have survived the shock, and so might the infant brother. . . .

PEGGY. Hugh!

O'CAHAN. If I hadn't missed a train by two minutes I'd have a profession to-day. If Uncle Hugh hadn't run to catch a train, he'd be in Rush Hill to-day and no auction.

PEGGY. You're only reciting every man's story, and many a woman's.

O'CAHAN. It's all blind and stupid and insolent. But one needn't quarrel with such despotism. . . . I'm going now, Peggy. If I don't see you again — good luck, good health, and good-bye [*He is going off, left*].

PEGGY. Just a moment, Hugh. Here's a clean collar. You look ghastly without a collar. . . .

O'CAHAN [*comes back*]. They say it's unlucky to turn back, but I'm in the position to take a risk. [*Putting on collar*] This is like dressing up a man before he goes out to be hanged.

PEGGY. I'll get you a clean handkerchief. [*She

gets one, rolls the jewellery in it and puts it in his breast pocket.]

O'CAHAN. Sing something, Peggy.

PEGGY. I don't feel like singing. Do you?

O'CAHAN. Certainly. [*Sings.*] " Down by the salley gardens my love and I did meet " . . .

PEGGY. Hugh O'Cahan, are you mad?

O'CAHAN. No, nor sad. You challenged me to sing.

PEGGY. God knows how men are built! I think if I were in your shoes this morning I'd drown myself.

O'CAHAN. A lot of good that would do. The old world would go on spinning as before. I don't suppose they'd postpone the auction. [*Putting on the tie*] I believe a great many people should be drowned at baptism. It would be their only chance of ever seeing the gates of Heaven, and 'twould save a lot of trouble down here later on. But there's no sense in letting a fellow grow up wild and then expect him to take a near-cut to the everlasting devil. I prefer Australia.

PEGGY. Don't talk wild, Hugh. You know I didn't mean it.

O'CAHAN. Are you afraid I might take a dip? You needn't. I'll die in my own comfortable bed at 103, surrounded by — that'll depend on what I've to leave the watchers. No cash — no tears, no prayers, no flowers. . . . How does this collar and tie sit me?

PEGGY. All right. They improve you.

O'CAHAN. Well, then, I'm off. Vale. [*He goes out left, singing.*] " She told me to take life easy, as the leaves grow on the tree " . . .

PEGGY [*listens*]. So ends it. [*She works quietly and shakes the water from her eyes.*] Vale.

MRS. SCALLY *comes in at the back; a sharp-looking woman, aged sixty, an ex-schoolmistress. She has a paper and some mail in her hand.*

MRS. SCALLY. Did I not hear voices, Peggy?

PEGGY. There's nobody here, mother. Is the post past?

MRS. SCALLY. Yes.

PEGGY. Nothing for me?

MRS. SCALLY. Nothing. [*Glancing at her*] You've been crying.

PEGGY. That's nothing new.

MRS. SCALLY. What have you got to cry about?

PEGGY. I don't really know. The tears just come, and then I let them come. It's very silly.

MRS. SCALLY. That blackguard O'Cahan is likely to come over here to say good-bye. He's going away after the auction. You mustn't see him.

PEGGY. Hugh O'Cahan is no blackguard! He's worth a gross of the people who've helped to drag him down.

MRS. SCALLY. Oh, indeed! Is that the way it is? Are you going to turn on me because he's left you in the lurch?

PEGGY. I'm sorry, mother. I shouldn't have spoken to you like that. But you mightn't try to hurt me. My three sisters can sneer quite enough without your assistance.

MRS. SCALLY. I said Hugh O'Cahan is a blackguard, and I repeat it.

PEGGY. What do you mean by a blackguard, mother?

B

MRS. SCALLY. A worthless prodigal.

PEGGY. O'Cahan's a fool. A fool to've gone in for horse-dealing with a pack of thieves. That's the worst can be said about him. If he were vicious would I ever have spoken to him?

MRS. SCALLY. Perhaps not — if you knew it. . . . When you finish what you're at, prepare the front bedroom. Your uncle has arrived in London from the Far East and is coming to see us. Professor Tim.

PEGGY. Pardon me, mother: you oughtn't to call him a professor. He isn't a real professor.

MRS. SCALLY. Well, of course, you with your convent training will know better than your mother. What, then, do you call him?

PEGGY. If he can be called anything in particular, it's a diviner.

MRS. SCALLY. Bless me! A diviner?

PEGGY. Yes, mother: a water-diviner. A person who can locate water with a hazel rod is called a diviner.

MRS. SCALLY. Well, while he remains here, he's a professor. That'll give the neighbours something to talk about.

PEGGY. I should say it will.

MRS. SCALLY. It's twenty years since he was last here. He was then studying Geology. If by this time he isn't a fully-fledged professor, I'll be astonished. I think you ought to feel rather pleased that your mother's only brother is a cut above the ordinary. Your father's people aren't much. Pig-dealers.

JOHN SCALLY *comes in, back; a sturdy little man with a thick brown beard, and ten years younger than his wife. He carries the salley switch with which he drove out the cows.*

JOHN. By the hokey, Bridget, this is grand news! Outrageous. When's Professor Tim coming?

MRS. SCALLY. The postcard doesn't say when. He's just arrived in London from the Far East, and may be here at any time.

JOHN. I'll be outrageous glad to see the Professor. Glad on your account, Bridget, and glad on his own. . . . But, three guesses: who's coming down our lane at this minute?

MRS. SCALLY. Himself! The Professor.

JOHN. Wrong, Bridget. Guess again.

MRS. SCALLY. Ach, don't annoy me! Who's coming?

JOHN. Mr. James J. Kilroy, the Rural Councillor, and his son Joseph. Hey! there's more news for you.

MRS. SCALLY. Don't lose your head, John. We owe the Kilroys nothing.

JOHN. They're driving. An atrocious fine pony and rubber-wheel trap. I wonder what they want here, Bridget. Such grand people.

MRS. SCALLY. They'll tell us that when they come in. If their grandeur frightens you, it doesn't frighten me. Go out and meet them and take them up to the hall door. And no scraping or touching your hat to them. Don't be a serf.

JOHN. You're a wonderful woman. [*Going.*] Outrageous.

MRS. SCALLY. Stop a minute. How often have I told you to stop using those two big words, outrageous and atrocious? Flinging them round you like paving-stones, and the whole parish laughing at you.

JOHN. It's just a habit, Bridget. Only a habit. I've done my level best to forget them, but they beat me. I must try again. [*He goes out.*]

MRS. SCALLY. Is the parlour tidy?

PEGGY. Yes, I dusted it and opened the windows.

MRS. SCALLY. Did you know these people were coming here?

PEGGY. I thought they might drop in going past to the auction.

MRS. SCALLY. Why, of course, that's it. They're going to the auction. Go and let them in.

PEGGY. Ah, mother, let them in yourself. I'm dirty.

MRS. SCALLY. So am I. But I'm clean enough for the Kilroys. [*She goes, left.*]

PEGGY. Now for the match-making. . . . [*Voices are heard in the yard. She looks out.*] Oh, holy father!

JOHN *ushers in at the back* JAMES KILROY *and his son* JOSEPH.

JOHN. The good-woman'll kill me for bringing you in the back door. She said I was to take you round to the front. We've a grand hall door, sir. Varnished and all. Outrageous.

KILROY. This is first-rate, John. Don't fret. Good morning, Miss Scally.

PEGGY. Good morning, Mr. Kilroy.

JOSEPH. Mornin', Peg.

PEGGY. Good morning, Joseph.

KILROY. I like to see a young woman at work early in the day. . . .

MRS. SCALLY *comes in*.

MRS. SCALLY. Good morning, everybody. I told John to take you round to the front, Mr. Kilroy. But you mightn't try to tell John anything.

KILROY. This is first-rate, Mrs. Scally. First-rate. [*Inspects it*.] Clean and neat and up-to-date. Sanitary.

MRS. SCALLY. Indeed it isn't clean at all. We must get the whole house cleaned from top to bottom, for my brother — the Professor — is going to pay us a visit. He's in London at present.

KILROY [*takes his hat off*]. I never knew you'd a brother a professor. I never heard of him.

MRS. SCALLY. Oh, indeed, yes. Tim's a professor. Won't you sit down?

KILROY. Thank you. [*Sits*.]

JOSEPH. I'll make myself at home over here. [*Sits on table and teases* PEGGY *awkwardly*.]

KILROY. This scoundrel O'Cahan, the bank's selling him up at last.

MRS. SCALLY. Yes, the auction's at eleven o'clock.

JOHN. Ay, as Bridget says, at eleven o'clock. Allison's the auctioneer. . . .

MRS. SCALLY. Silence, John. [*To* KILROY] He has nothing left to sell but the land. Not a four-footed animal about the house. . .

PEGGY. Excuse me, Joseph. [*She goes out, back*.]

JOSEPH. Will I go with ye, Peg? [*No answer*.] I'll risk it. [*He goes out*.]

MRS. SCALLY [*surmising something*]. Joseph's getting a fine young man.

JOHN. Outrageous.

KILROY. Between ourselves, Joseph's a bit of a

playboy. No real vice, you know, but reckless and wild and full of animal spirits. I sent him to an agricultural college, but they couldn't subdue him. He put himself at the head of a band of gentlemen's sons and half-wrecked the college, and then wrecked the town.

MRS. SCALLY [*laughs*]. I wouldn't think a thing of that. Students are full of mischief.

JOHN. Ay, as Bridget says, full of life. Fine fellows, Mr. Kilroy. Atrocious.

KILROY. Now, John Scally, I want no more " mistering ". You and I kneel in the same church, and after myself you're the best respected people in the parish. Call me James.

MRS. SCALLY. That's what I like to hear. No pride or nonsense.

KILROY. I'm going over to this auction. What condition's the place in, John? I haven't been up at Rush Hill for years.

JOHN. The sun never warmed a better place, James. Two hundred acres like a carrot-bed. You could sow at Christmas.

KILROY. I know the land's good. But what about the house? They tell me it's in ruins.

JOHN. It's not in very good re——

MRS. SCALLY. Silence, John. . . . The house inside is in ruins, James. O'Cahan had a band of ruffians like himself playing cards there, and they burnt down the stairs and most of the woodwork. . . .

JOHN. For firewood, James . . . as Bridget can tell you.

KILROY. Well, to come to the point. The bank has four thousand pounds again it, and — but this is very private — the bank wants me to buy it.

MRS. SCALLY. Buy it, James. Buy it. You'll never rue the day you bought Rush Hill. Only that we bought a second farm last year, we'd buy it ourselves.

JOHN. Buy it, James, as Bridget says——

MRS. SCALLY. Silence, John. [*To* KILROY] Buy it, James.

KILROY. I've a plan in my head, Mrs. Scally, and I'll submit it to you, for I've a deal of faith in your judgement.

MRS. SCALLY. Thank you, James. Whatever you say here is private.

KILROY. I know that, or I wouldn't broach it. A public man has to know who he's talking to.

MRS. SCALLY. Very true.

JOHN. As Bridget says, very true.

KILROY. We were speaking about my son Joseph. He's twenty-one years old this morning.

MRS. SCALLY. Bless him, I didn't think he was near that age.

JOHN. Amen. I didn't think he was sixteen.

KILROY. Joseph comes into his legacy this morning, two thousand pounds: his aunt's money that died ten years ago.

MRS. SCALLY. God guard him, it's a lot of money.

JOHN. Amen. As Bridget says, it's a mint.

KILROY. Pay good attention, both of you, to what follows. It seems Joseph attended a Gaelic class last winter in somebody's barn.

MRS. SCALLY. In Cassidy's barn. Peggy was there too.

KILROY. The story goes that Joseph noticed Peggy there and became attracted by her.

MRS. SCALLY. We never heard that before.

JOHN. We never did, sir, or we mightn't have allowed it.

MRS. SCALLY. Silence, John. I didn't mean it in that sense. Peggy Scally's good enough for any young man in the parish to speak to. I only said we didn't know that she and Joseph were friendly, and we didn't.

KILROY. Shake hands, Bridget. [*They shake.*] I agree with every word you say. Peggy Scally's a match for the best young man in this constituency — and that happens to be my son Joseph. I hope that's not bragging.

JOHN. Yah! [*Displeased.*]

MRS. SCALLY [*smiling*]. You put that very well, James. I read all your speeches at the Council, and you always hit the nail on the head.

KILROY. Thank you, Bridget. I'm ten years a member of the Council Board, and that's the first bit of criticism that ever entirely pleased me. You're a brainy woman, Bridget.

JOHN. Yah!

KILROY. Now, prepare yourselves for a shock. Joseph last night told his mother and me, plump and plain, that he means to marry Peggy Scally or die in the attempt.

MRS. SCALLY. Goodness gracious me! That's a bombshell. [*Letting herself go*] Mercy save us again. . . . I'm dizzy. . . . John, d'ye hear what he says?

JOHN. Yah!

KILROY. At first his mother — and indeed myself — objected most strenuously. But he's a Kilroy. He gave us till this morning to consent, or hand him out his two thousand pounds. That's the sort of young man Joseph is.

MRS. SCALLY [*on her dignity*]. May we ask, Mr. Kilroy, why you and Mrs. Kilroy objected so strenuously to the match?

JOHN. Hey! that's a good question. Outrageous.

KILROY. And a very natural question. But when I submit the reason I know you'll appreciate it. His mother and myself both understood that Peggy was engaged to Hugh O'Cahan.

JOHN. Yah! [*Sulks again.*]

MRS. SCALLY. There never was anything serious between Peggy and Hugh O'Cahan, and I as strenuously objected to anything that might have been.

KILROY. That answer satisfies me entirely. I told Mrs. Kilroy it was only a rumour. But she was uneasy. You see the legacy come by her sister. Rachel.

MRS. SCALLY. Well, till your wife comes over here and tells me out of her own mouth that she's satisfied, there will be no match — not if Joseph had a million.

JOHN. Hey, James! what do you think of that? This lady of mine doesn't mince matters.

KILROY. I didn't expect this, Bridget. But it has to be met. When the Council gets into a fix I have to get them out of it. [*Ponders.*] What's the matter with you, Bridget, coming to our house and discussing it with Mrs. Kilroy? I'll give you all the assistance in my power.

MRS. SCALLY. I'll want no assistance, James, for I won't go.

JOHN. Hey!

KILROY [*slowly*]. Well, maybe I'll be able to manage Mrs. Kilroy myself. You know what a mother is, Bridget, where her oldest son is concerned. She maybe had something bigger in her eye for Joseph.

MRS. SCALLY. She may've had something bigger in her eye, but she'd nothing better than Peggy Scally. And please tell your wife I said so.

JOHN. Holy tattler! that's the best yet. Honour where honour's due. Outrageous.

KILROY. You're making it very hard for me, Bridget. You've no conception of my difficulty——

MRS. SCALLY. There needn't be any difficulty at all, James. If my daughter's not good enough for your wife, there's no harm done. And if your wife's coming to see me, bring her to-night; for the Professor may be here to-morrow and he mightn't want to meet strangers.

KILROY [*slaps his leg*]. That's the solution of the problem! There's no problem without a solution. Mrs. Kilroy has a weakness for distinguished people. She'll want to hear all about the Professor from your own lips. What time to-night, Bridget, would suit your convenience?

MRS. SCALLY. About six.

KILROY. She'll come in that door on the stroke of six. And now for the next item. If Joseph and Peggy make a match of it, what about Rush Hill? O'Cahan's house and two hundred acres, eh?

JOHN [*gasps*]. Rush Hill!

MRS. SCALLY. James Kilroy, I'll say it: You're a big, bold, clear-headed man.

KILROY. Is it only now you're finding that out, Bridget? The people for years have been saying it.

MRS. SCALLY. I always knew you had ability. Your wife has none.

KILROY. Quite right, Bridget. And your husband has none. No offence, John.

JOHN. Lord no, James! Nothing in that to take offence at. I never put up to've ability. I'd no need of ability: I've always made my living with my hands and feet.

KILROY. Well, we know now where we are. The next is only a question of money. If I buy Rush Hill, Bridget, will you stock it?

JOHN. That's one for you, Bridget.

MRS. SCALLY. That's a very important item, James. It would take five or six hundred pounds to stock it.

KILROY. It would take five. Could you give Peggy that sum without hurting yourself? It would mean big matches for your other daughters.

JOHN. Yah!

MRS. SCALLY. It might. But if we give Peggy five hundred pounds, my other daughters might expect the same, and I couldn't afford it. . . . Tell me this, James. If Joseph's legacy buys Rush Hill, where do you come in? You wouldn't be out a penny.

JOHN. Hey! that's one for you, James.

KILROY. Joseph's legacy won't wink at buying it; we'll be very snug if another thousand buys it. The difference I must raise myself, or go security for it.

MRS. SCALLY. Well, buy it, James, and we'll stock it. I want to see Peggy and Joseph in Rush Hill.

KILROY [*gets up and wipes his forehead*]. I'd no idea that arranging a match was so difficult. It's a terrible strain. [*Looks at his watch.*] You'll come with me, John, to the auction, and we'll look about us before it begins.

JOHN. I'd as lief not go near it, James. I hate these auction-outs.

MRS. SCALLY. Silence, John. Get your good coat and hat.

JOHN. The neighbours are going to boycott it.

KILROY. All the better for us, John.

JOHN. Let us all boycott it.

KILROY. No, but let us go and bid a wicked bad price, then I can deal with the bank on my own terms.

MRS. SCALLY. James Kilroy, I'll speak out what's in my mind. You're the best business man in the parish, and I'm married to the worst. . . .

JOHN. Ah, Bridget, Bridget! that's shockin' unfair. . . .

KILROY. I don't want to boast, Bridget, but [*expanding his chest*] if I'd got a woman of your calibre this parish wouldn't have held me.

MRS. SCALLY. I'm certain of it.

JOHN. Ah, by the holy, that's cruelty to animals! Where's my hat and coat, Bridget?

MRS. SCALLY. I'll get them for you. Come into the room, James. I want to treat you. . . . Come along, John.

JOHN. Ay, at your heel!

They are going when JOSEPH *and* PEGGY *come in arm in arm.*

JOSEPH. Hi! look at this. You're missing all the sights.

KILROY [*turning*]. Good man, Joseph! He's won her. He's a Kilroy. You couldn't stop the breed with a mountain battery.

MRS. SCALLY. Mercy, the cheek of young people

nowadays! Aren't you pair ashamed of yourselves?

JOSEPH. We glory in it. Huroo!

KILROY [shouts]. He's a Kilroy! Thunder and lightning couldn't daunt the breed. Didn't you wreck the college, Joseph?

JOSEPH. Ay, and the town it was in.

KILROY. Will we buy Rush Hill, Joseph?

JOSEPH. You'll buy it and I'll pay it!

KILROY. Well put, Joseph. And Peggy's mother'll stock it.

JOSEPH. Well put again. Go on, now, and leave us alone.

MRS. SCALLY [laughing]. He's a Kilroy all right. . . . Come on, James and John; we're not wanted here. [She and KILROY and JOHN go out.]

JOSEPH. It's all settled, Peggy. We're as good as married. Amn't I a hero?

PEGGY [removing his arm]. Yes, and a modest soul. [Takes up iron.]

JOSEPH [sheepishly]. Awh, Peggy . . . awh, now. Just one. Gwon.

PEGGY. Just one what?

JOSEPH. Awh, you know yourself. . . . It starts with a K.

PEGGY. Gracious, I think I know what you mean. What an awful suggestion! What would your mother say, Joseph?

JOSEPH. Awh, sure she wouldn't know.

PEGGY. But she might suspect. Better not risk it, Joseph.

JOSEPH [drawing closer]. Awh, let her . . . let her suspect.

PEGGY. Mind the iron, Joseph. It's hot.

JOSEPH [tries to kiss her and leaps in the air]. Livin'

Moses! I'm roasted. [*Licks his hand.*]

PEGGY. I'm sorry, Joseph. I told you 'twas hot.

JOSEPH. Awh, what do I care about a burn? I'd ram my hand into the flames of the fire. . . .

PEGGY. You're fearfully wild, Joseph.

JOSEPH. Awh, you'll soon tame me. Tell me again, Peggy. Isn't all over between you and O'Cahan?

PEGGY. Well, I haven't quite forgotten him yet.

JOSEPH. Awh, you'll soon forget all about him. You'll soon think of nothing in the world but me. O'Cahan was a rap. . . .

O'CAHAN *stalks in, back. He has the packet in one hand and whip in the other.*

O'CAHAN. Your presents, Peggy [*throws packet on table*]. I found them in my pocket. Make jam of them. [*Wheels on* JOSEPH] Who's a rap?

JOSEPH [*cowering*]. Mind, my father's in the room!

O'CAHAN. Call him out.

JOSEPH. If you touch me I'll soon call him. . . .

O'CAHAN [*hits him a scud with whip*]. There! call out the Rural Councillor.

JOSEPH [*backing away*]. I want no fighting——

O'CAHAN. No, you're a Kilroy. You burn down colleges and paint towns red in your sleep. For two straws I'd put a lip on you!

JOSEPH. My father'll writ ye! He'll writ ye! You'll not hit me again with a whip. . . .

O'CAHAN. Call him out. I'll put a lip on him too.

PEGGY. Hugh, for goodness' sake don't make a scene. It isn't worth it.

JOSEPH [*hugging room door*]. You'll see my father

at the auction. He'll buy you up, stump and rump.

O'CAHAN. And who'll pay for it?

JOSEPH. I'll pay! I'm into my legacy this morning. Two thousand gold sovereigns!

O'CAHAN. Listen to me, gurnet. Your father's
been swelling about on that money for the last ten
years. You'll have fun getting your two thousand
pounds, or I'm a fish. That's why he brought you
here this morning — to stop your mouth with a
woman. [*To* PEGGY] Now, Peggy, there's more
news for you. You've broken with a bankrupt man
to marry a bankrupt prig.

JOSEPH. Awh, you'll see that at the auction!

PROFESSOR TIM *comes in at the back; an oldish man,
in seafaring clothes, with the appearance of a toper.*

PROFESSOR [*swaying a little on his legs*]. Hullo!
How's all here?

PEGGY. All well, thank you. Do you take meal
or only coppers?

PROFESSOR. I take neither meal nor coppers,
sweetheart. But you can gimme a kiss if you
like. . . .

O'CAHAN [*reaching for him, but stops*]. Eh? That
old face of yours looks rather homely.

PROFESSOR. And your fist, mister, looks awful
homely to me. You draw out to scatter a man like
an O'Cahan, of Rush Hill.

O'CAHAN. That's me.

PROFESSOR. Sorry, mister. Your pony and trap's
in trouble down the lane. It's turned turtle in a
ditch.

JOSEPH. It's mine . . . mine! [*He runs out.*]

PROFESSOR [*looking about*]. I wonder to Gawd am

I in the wrong shop after all! Whose bungalow's this?

O'CAHAN. You're all right, Professor. This is John Scally's bungalow. . . .

PEGGY. What! Professor? Oh, sacred trust!

PROFESSOR. Whoa, gal. Don't be so obvious. [*To* O'CAHAN] Who's this exclamatory female?

O'CAHAN. Your own niece, Professor. Miss Peggy Scally.

PROFESSOR. Hullo, sweetheart! Begum, I've travelled seven times round the world and never seen a sweeter face. [*Hobbling closer.*] Shake hands, pigeon, with Uncle Tim. The old Professor . . .

PEGGY. Go away! Keep back! [*Screams.*] Mother! Mother!

MRS. SCALLY *comes in.*

PROFESSOR. Hullo, sister Bridget. Begum, you haven't aged an hour. Re-markable.

MRS. SCALLY [*stunned*]. Aaaaaaaah!

O'CAHAN. Sister Bridget doesn't seem to recognize you, Professor. You must have changed a bit since you were last here.

PROFESSOR. Changed? Begum, man, I've been near dead a dozen times. Malaria in Nigeria, yellow-jack in Panama, snake-bite in Siam, and various other accidents by land and sea——

O'CAHAN. And liquor.

PROFESSOR. No, no. I never touch it. I'm a soda-water fountain. [*Chuckles.*] Accidents by land and sea and soda water.

MRS. SCALLY. So after raking the gutters of the world you've come back to see us?

PROFESSOR. Only to pay my respects, Bridget.

Why, it must be twenty years since I looked you up. . . .

MRS. SCALLY. Well, you've seen me, and I've seen you. Let that do you for the rest of your life. There's the door. Step out and don't come back. We harbour no rakes here — young or old.

PROFESSOR [*astonished*]. Begum, this is a surprise. This is a nice reception to give the Professor brother after a lifetime abroad. It's downright uncivil.

O'CAHAN. A little chilly. . . .

PROFESSOR. A *little* chilly? Mister, it's an iceberg.

MRS. SCALLY. Master Hugh, if you don't hurry home you won't be in time for the auction.

O'CAHAN. Thank you. I'm just going. . . . I'm not as far down as I thought. [*He goes out.*]

MRS. SCALLY. Now, you ruffian! what brought you here in that condition?

PROFESSOR. Don't ask double-barrelled questions. My object in coming here, and the condition I arrive in, are two different things. Take it point by point.

MRS. SCALLY. What brought you here at all?

PROFESSOR. For a holiday. A complete rest.

MRS. SCALLY. Well, you've chosen the wrong place: you won't find rest here. Go and take a holiday in the gutter. [*Points to the door*] Step out and disappear. . . .

PROFESSOR [*manages to sit on the table*]. I'm awful tired. I've been travelling a deal lately.

MRS. SCALLY [*exasperated*]. Will you step out — before I pitch you out?

PROFESSOR. Pitch me out? You didn't pitch me out the morning you married Johnny Scally . . . when I laid a hundred pounds in your lap. Why,

C

bust you, 'twas that hundred pounds gave you and
Johnny a start.

MRS. SCALLY [*on a new tack*]. I'll give you a few
shillings and you'll catch the first train. My family
are all grown up and you wouldn't want to affront us.

PROFESSOR. I'm not going to affront anybody.
All I want is a quiet holiday along the bog-edges.
. . . I want to pick a little white heather.

JOHN, *in black coat and hat, comes in, followed by*
KILROY. MRS. SCALLY *stands in front of the* PRO-
FESSOR *to screen him*.

KILROY. Where's Joseph?

PEGGY. He ran down the lane. Something happened to the pony. . . .

PROFESSOR. It's turned turtle in a ditch.

KILROY. Dang it all! [*He flings out*.]

PROFESSOR [*pushes* MRS. SCALLY *away*]. Stand away
back! What are you crowding me up for?

JOHN. Bridget, who the hedges is this?

PROFESSOR. Hullo, Johnny! Begum, you stand
the years like a brass button. Greetings.

JOHN. By holy, it's the Professor! Lord save us,
such a case! Such a wreck!

PROFESSOR. Johnny, don't be so obvious. A man
after a long journey doesn't look his best. I'm tired.

JOHN. Ah, poor Tim. . . .

MRS. SCALLY. There! not another word. . . .

JOHN. Ah, Bridget, let me shake his hand——

MRS. SCALLY. Silence! He's going out of this.
I'll give him a few shillings and he'll catch the first
train away. He can't stay here.

PROFESSOR. I won't catch no train away, sister.
I'm too glad to be home. I want a wash-up, and a

good feed of spuds and cabbage, and about a week's
sleep.   I'm so tired.

MRS. SCALLY [*grabbing his arm*]. Come with me!
I'll show you what you're going to get. . . .

PROFESSOR [*resisting*]. Let me go! I won't budge
an inch.

MRS. SCALLY. Come on, John, lend a hand. We'll
get him outside.

JOHN. I'd rather not, Bridget.

MRS. SCALLY. Come on — when you're told! Or
I'll smash you too.

JOHN [*assists*]. Come now, Tim. Come, like a
good fellow. I wouldn't for the whole world hurt
a hair of your head.

PEGGY. Mother, mother! the Kilroys are coming in.

MRS. SCALLY. Come, John. Quick. We must
keep them outside. [*She and* JOHN *go out.*]

PROFESSOR. Hullo, Peggy. Who did you say was
coming — the police?

PEGGY. Not at all: two neighbours.

PROFESSOR [*musing*]. Begum, I've touched low-
water mark at last. Taken by the scruff of the neck
like a rat to be thrown out. [*Sobs and watches the
effect on* PEGGY.] It's hard to be old and frail and
homeless and penniless and friendless. [*Drying his
eyes*] That's what family relations amount to. . . .
No matter. . . . Eaten bread's forgotten.

PEGGY. Never mind, uncle.

PROFESSOR. Eh? Your voice is kind. Calling me
uncle, are you?

PEGGY. Yes, why not?

PROFESSOR. Plenty of why-nots. I'm a returned
empty, that's the main why-not.

PEGGY [*impulsively*]. Empty or full, rich or poor, you're my Uncle Tim. [*Shaking hands*] You're welcome home, uncle.

PROFESSOR. Thanks, pigeon. You've got a heart. Your kind voice I'll remember till I die. Any more sisters, Peggy?

PEGGY. Three sisters and three brothers.

PROFESSOR. Where are they?

PEGGY. They're over at the other farm making hay.

PROFESSOR. Have you two farms now?

PEGGY. Yes, we bought a second farm last year.

PROFESSOR. Begum, your father deserves credit. He got a tartar of a wife. A proper shrew.

PEGGY. Oh, mother isn't bad. She just likes to boss a little.

PROFESSOR. That's obvious. An impossible woman. A victim of temper, vocabulary, and spleen. Do you remember me being here before, Peggy?

PEGGY. Quite well, uncle. You brought me a string of blue beads.

PROFESSOR. Did I? I'm glad. I don't remember a thing about it. Bad memory. [*Looks at his empty hands*] I thought all the time I'd a valise in my hand. Have I no personal baggage at all?

PEGGY. None with you.

PROFESSOR. I must have dropped it in Paris or London. . . . I'm coming from Nigeria, Peggy. Been coming by easy stages for months and months. [*Looks at his clothes*] I wonder to Gawd where I got this toggery. Looks like seafaring clothes. . . . Probably got them by mistake in London.

PEGGY. When did you arrive in Ireland, uncle?

PROFESSOR. I haven't the remotest idea. The last

thing I remember is being down at the docks in London. What day is this, Peggy?

PEGGY. Monday.

PROFESSOR. What date is it?

PEGGY. The 6th of July.

PROFESSOR. July? Why, I thought 'twas May. There's a big gap somewhere. The whole month of June is blotted out.

PEGGY. You've been drinking, uncle.

PROFESSOR. Not a great deal, Peggy; just enjoying myself. . . . I say, Peggy, will your mother put me out?

PEGGY. I'm afraid so.

PROFESSOR. So am I. And you're my only hope. Could you give me a little cash? About five pounds. I'm dead broke.

PEGGY. I could give you three pounds, uncle. It's all the money I've got.

PROFESSOR. Well, for Gawd's sake, hurry up and get it.

PEGGY. One minute. [*She goes to the room.*]

PROFESSOR [*looks all round the kitchen*]. This is a comfortable spot. A wandering man could find rest here. [*Recites:*]

" And, as an hare, whom horns and hounds pursue,
    Pants to the place from whence at first she flew,
    I still had hopes, my long vexations pass'd,
    Here to return — and die at home at last."

What an autobiography I could give the young Scallys, if that woman would let me stay here. A man with the dust of forty countries on his shoes.

PEGGY *comes in with the money.*

PEGGY. Three pounds, uncle. Don't let on to mother.

PROFESSOR [*taking it*]. No fear, Peggy. She'd put me down and take it from me. [*Takes out snuff-box.*] Have a pinch. Jockey Club.

PEGGY. Gracious heavens! is that the smell was taking the breath from me. . . . Don't let mother see it.

PROFESSOR. Does your mother not take snuff?

PEGGY. Don't let her see it, I tell you.

PROFESSOR [*takes snuff*]. It clears the head, Peggy. It actually sobers a man. I feel better already. If your mother wasn't so hostile I could stay here for years. Would you mind, Peggy?

PEGGY. Not if you behaved yourself. . . .

MRS. SCALLY *comes in, very warlike.*

MRS. SCALLY. Are you still here?

PROFESSOR. Where did you think I'd be? Evaporated?

MRS. SCALLY. Have you no spirit left?

PROFESSOR. I've too much spirit. I'm all spirit. What I want is a little more physical ability.

MRS. SCALLY. Oh, you prodigal you! You vagabond! That the very smell of the house is abominable. . . .

PEGGY. It's only snuff, mother. If you leave him to me he'll give no trouble. I'll get him something to eat and he'll rest and go away.

MRS. SCALLY. He'll never break bread in my house! He'll never sleep under my roof! God only knows where he's coming from or what plague he has with him.

PROFESSOR. My only plague is poverty. A

chronic attack of penury. It arises from an absence of brass in the vest pocket. And at my age it's incurable.

JOHN *comes in.*

JOHN. Now, Tim, your own sister won't have you here. I've got my orders to shift you. It's not a nice job, but I'm only carrying out orders. Come now, like a good fella. I'll drive you in to the station and buy you a ticket for some big town.

PROFESSOR. You won't let me stay for even one night?

MRS. SCALLY. No. You're not fit to be in human habitation. [*Sniffs.*] You're poisonous.

PROFESSOR. I'm a sick man, a broken man.

MRS. SCALLY. Not too sick to come here and affront us . . . you prodigal!

JOHN. Easy now, Bridget. It's a fearful thing to turn your face away from a broken man. . . . We're all prodigals . . . and we must all crawl back some day——

MRS. SCALLY. Silence, you! It's me is turning him out. He'll not be in my house!

PROFESSOR [*struggling to his feet*]. All right, sister. I'm going. I can crawl back the road I came. . . .

MRS. SCALLY. John'll drive you to the station and see you off. You're not going to affront us crawling along the road in that condition.

PROFESSOR [*draws a seaman's knife*]. Let you and Johnny mind your own business. If anybody tries to stop me I'll defend myself. [*He is going out at the back.*]

MRS. SCALLY. Don't let him out, John! Stop him!

JOHN. By the hokey, I'll do no such thing. That

man would think little of knifing me. He's a sailor.

PEGGY [*goes to* PROFESSOR *at the door*]. Give me that knife, uncle. Please.

PROFESSOR. Sorry, pigeon. I couldn't get along without it. It's the knife I cut my food and baccy with.

PEGGY. Well, put it in your pocket. Nobody's going to stop you. You'll come with me to the old kitchen, and I'll get you something to eat.

MRS. SCALLY. Never!

PEGGY. Mother, I'll feed him. Nobody knows whose turn it may be next.

JOHN. God bless you, Peggy. Feed him, and let him rest his bones.

PROFESSOR *puts knife in his pocket.* KILROY *and* JOSEPH *come in. They stand staring at him.*

PROFESSOR. Bless you, pigeon. You're as good as you look. I'll go with you like a lamb.

PEGGY. Come on, then. I'll help you across. [*She and* PROFESSOR *go out.*]

KILROY. Who's that ould viper? I seem to know his face. [*Sniffing.*] The smell of whiskey and snuff and rotten fish would poison you!

MRS. SCALLY. It's not drink, James. He's a poor man, with the palsy or something, and Peggy always feeds him in the old kitchen.

KILROY. The Lord know how she does it! She'll surely get a powerful reward in Heaven. For I couldn't go near him.

JOSEPH. I could go near him! I'll go and give him a penny. . . .

MRS. SCALLY. No, Joseph, you mustn't go near him. He doesn't like strangers.

KILROY. John, are we going to this auction? If we are it's time we were away. We won't have a minute to look about us. . . .

MRS. SCALLY. Go, in God's name, and buy it. I'm determined to see Peggy and Joseph in Rush Hill.

JOSEPH. So am I! Come on, father. [*He goes out.*]

KILROY. He's a Kilroy! [*Goes out.*]

JOHN [*calls after him*]. I'll follow you in a minute, James. [*To* MRS. SCALLY] Don't you turn out that unfortunate till I come back.

MRS. SCALLY. Why not?

JOHN. Because it's not right. It's not Christian. It's not human. Tim gave us a fine start the morning we were married.

MRS. SCALLY. You've a very long memory.

JOHN. And you've a very short one.

MRS. SCALLY. Step on. He'll not be here.

JOHN. If you turn him out he'll die on the road.

MRS. SCALLY. If he does we can bury him. Step on.

JOHN. I may go. But not in God's name. I'm not enough of a Scribe and Pharisee for that. We couldn't have luck after this day's work. We don't deserve it.

MRS. SCALLY. Leave my own brother to me. He won't be here when you come back. I'll drive him to the station myself and ship him. . . .

JOHN. Uncharitable woman. . . . [*He goes out.*]

MRS. SCALLY [*sniffing*]. Mercy! the smell of this house . . . like rotten fish. [*She opens the doors and windows.*] If the Kilroys find out who he is — that's an end to everything.

PEGGY *comes in shaking her head.*

PEGGY. We're lost, mother. He's gone off across the fields to the auction.

MRS. SCALLY [*shrieks*]. The auction! Why did you let him out!

PEGGY. Because I couldn't keep him in. He threatened me with the knife. The man's either an eccentric or a plain madman.

MRS. SCALLY [*sinks on a chair*]. Oh, Lord above! Am I to be persecuted and afflicted off the face of the earth? Or why do You permit these people — one and all of them — to make my life a misery! Why, why?

Curtain

ACT II

o'cahan's *dining-room. Tall windows look out on the lawn. A heavy panelled door leads to the hall.*

The room has a tumble-down appearance. There are prints of race-horses, jockeys, and a large portrait of o'cahan's *deceased uncle on the walls. A few silver cups and other trophies are on the sideboard.*

MOLL FLANAGAN, *a squat, middle-aged maid, is up on a chair trying to hang a clean curtain. The sky has darkened and the bluish light suggests rain.*

MOLL. Och, hum, anee oh! May the curse of Cain fall on the man or woman that comes to the auction, and may they roast for ever in eternal torment that buys it over his unfortunate head! [*Fights with the curtain.*] Blast ye, stay where I put ye!

o'cahan *comes in and looks around for a book.*

o'cahan. Well, Moll, are you spring cleaning?

MOLL. I'm trying to make it a trifle dacent-looking, dear.

o'cahan. I think the shutters would be more suitable.

MOLL. We'll keep a bold front as long as we can.

o'cahan. But aren't you foolish to hang clean curtains for somebody else?

MOLL. God look to your wit if you think I'm hanging them for somebody else! It's for our own bit of respect and dacency. I'll soon tear them down after the auction.

o'cahan. Suit yourself, Moll. You're the house-keeper.

moll. And I'll tear down more than the curtains. I'll not leave a whole pane of glass in the house, nor a square inch of plaster on the walls that I won't smash off with the hatchet. And they'll be lucky if I don't burn it to the ground.

o'cahan. No vandalism, Moll. Don't you see him watching you?

moll. Who's watching me?

o'cahan [points to portrait]. Uncle Hugh. If you start smashing things he'll maybe speak to you.

moll. God knows, he's speaking to me all the time, and his eyes following me everywhere. Hide the hatchet then, the way I won't see it in my rage.

o'cahan. Did you happen to see a small book with a green cover lying around? Lindsay Gordon's poems.

moll. I'm sure it's burnt. I've been lighting the fire with books for three days.

o'cahan. If I saw you lighting the fire with a book, Moll, I'd put you in the oven. [Finds the book.] Here it is, Moll. [Opens at random and reads:]

" Life is mostly froth and bubble.
    Two things stand like stone:
    Kindness in another's trouble,
    Courage in your own."

That bucks a fellow up, Moll.

moll. The uncle — God be gracious to him — was dying about that same book. He'd yards of it on his tongue.

o'cahan [turning the leaves]. I'm looking for

something with a good kick in it. Listen to this,
Moll. [*Reads:*]

" She passed like an arrow Kildare and Cock
          Sparrow,
    And Mantrap and Mermaid refused the stone wall;
    And Giles on the Grayling came down at the
          paling,
    And I was left sailing in front of them all."

MOLL. Many a time I heard the uncle at that bit.
But this was his great favourite, and he'd rhyme it
over fifty times a day. [*She half sings it:*]

" She rose when I hit her, I saw the stream glitter,
    A wide scarlet nostril flashed close to my knee;
    Between sky and water the Clown came and caught
          her,
    The space that he cleared was a caution to see."

Fancy that now. Passing him in mid-air going over
the water-lep.

O'CAHAN [*laughing*]. Go on, Moll. One other
spasm. It does me good to hear you.

MOLL. God knows, I'd make a fool of myself to
hear your laugh. [*She recites:*]

" She raced at the rasper, I felt my knees grasp her,
    I found my hands give to her strain on the bit;
    She rose when the Clown did — our silks as we
          bounded,
    Brushed lightly, our stirrups clashed loud as we
          hit."

O'CAHAN. Thank you, Moll. If I find myself at
Lindsay Gordon's grave, I'll put an extra flower on
it for Moll Flanagan.

MOLL. And say a prayer for me, too. I'm sure he was an Irish poet-maker.

O'CAHAN. Very like. Now, is Paddy Kinney never back from town?

MOLL [*looks out window*]. He's coming up the avenue at this precise minute, and he with a basket in every hand.

O'CAHAN. If you want me I'll be in the kitchen, reading bits of Gordon to the Professor.

MOLL. Well, all I can say is — you're ill off for a job. For I never seen a monument of desolation like that man walking the world. What's he a professor av? What does he profess to be?

O'CAHAN. Theology.

MOLL. And do they give him nothing to live upon? He's in ruins. He's like a rat-catcher.

PADDY KINNEY, *an elderly groom, comes in. He has various parcels, including a paper bag with a lady's hat.*

O'CAHAN. Well, Paddy, you seem to've raised the wind again. You're laden like a bee in June.

PADDY. Raised the wind, is it? My sowl, your credit's as good as the Bank of Ireland. I could finance a new railway by naming your name.

O'CAHAN. It would be a very short railway, Paddy, and a very narrow gauge. But never mind. What have you home with you?

PADDY. I've both money and value, boss. Wait till you see them baskets in the hall and they packed with corn-beef, cakes, and porter galore.

O'CAHAN. Many people gathering down at the road?

PADDY. Very few. Just big, blustering Kilroy, with the son Joe at his fut — like a spent foal —

and John Scally. I suppose the wife made John toe the line.

O'CAHAN. Call me when the auctioneer comes. I'll be in the kitchen. [*He goes out.*]

PADDY [*bitterly*]. Scoff and roast the town of Ballykennedy! That I may live to see nettles fourteen feet high growing in the main street. The people he spent hundreds of pounds with wouldn't gimme a pot of jam without the money.

MOLL. How then did you get all the provisions you've home with you?

PADDY. I paid for them myself with my own bit of savings. Ten pounds I'd past me for a rainy day. Twenty years' gathering.

MOLL [*comes from window*]. Did you get me anything for my head?

PADDY. I got you a hat. And a dress. That's what kept me so long — choosing them. I'll never undertake a work of the kind again if I live for ever.

MOLL [*excited*]. Show me the hat, Paddy. Quick.

PADDY. You'll put the dress on first. You wouldn't want to put the dress on over the hat, would you? Like putting a bridle on a horse before the saddle. [*He opens a parcel and takes out a red dress with black spots.*]

MOLL. I don't like it!

PADDY. Blessed and holy Moses! You don't like it?

MOLL. I never liked red.

PADDY. Because you never had no taste. Weren't you and your clothes always a fright? Here, on with it now.

MOLL [*takes dress*]. Go you out of the room before I on with it.

PADDY. Gwon, get into it! I'm not looking at you at all. I've something else in my mind at this minute than your figure.

MOLL. Well, turn your back, Paddy, like a dacent man.

PADDY [*goes to window*]. Blast you and your modesty! You'd think you were sixteen. Hurry up now, or I'll wheel on you.

MOLL [*puts dress on*]. All right, Paddy. You can turn round now.

PADDY [*turns*]. It's a pome. You're like the pillar of fire that walked before Moses.

MOLL [*twisting*]. How does it look at the back?

PADDY. Could you not tighten the girths a little?

MOLL [*tightening it*]. It should have a belt. . . . Is that better?

PADDY. I asked the shopkeeper if there wasn't a surcingle, and he said surcingles are out of fashion.

MOLL [*trying to look at her heels*]. How does it look round at the back, Paddy?

PADDY. Jog across there a few paces.

MOLL. Lord, it's not a horse you're vittin'.

PADDY. How then can I see your back if you don't give me a show? Jog on. [MOLL *obeys.*] Woah! Stand up straight. Now, draw yourself well up and shorten your stride a little. . . . Come on. . . . Woah! It has just one fault ; it's far too stylish for the likes of you.

MOLL [*pleased*]. Oh, that's a good fault. I'll keep it. Now, let me see the hat.

PADDY [*takes out a bilious-looking hat entwined with varnished cherries*]. Put that on your head now, and then look in the glass.

MOLL. Oh, it's a beauty! I like the hat, Paddy. But I haven't a hat-pin.

PADDY. There you are. Two of them. [*Hands her two long pins with black heads.*]

MOLL [*putting hat on*]. God knows, Paddy Kinney, you're a marvel. You forget nothing.

PADDY. A man that's looked after leppin' horses for twenty years doesn't forget much.

MOLL. And to be a man you're tasty.

PADDY. A man that's attended Dublin Horse Show for twenty years should know when a woman's groomed.

MOLL. Wait till I see how it looks. [*Goes to a mirror and stands twisting her neck.*]

PADDY. Take care you don't twist your neck out of joint. . . . My God, the vanity of wimin!

MOLL [*turning*]. Isn't it gorgeous, Paddy?

PADDY. You've left me without a word to say. It's a pome.

MOLL. I'm well pleased with everything. What did they cost, Paddy?

PADDY. They cost you nothing at all. They're an acknowledgement for all the imperence and washing and patching you've done for me. . . . Your health to wear them.

MOLL. Ah, Paddy, Paddy——

PADDY. Not another word now. It's our last day under this roof, and you can face the world now well groomed and respectable. In that rig you'll have no trouble getting new service.

MOLL. Whisht!

O'CAHAN *and* PROFESSOR *come in.*

PROFESSOR. Hullo, Paddy Kinney. Begum, I'd

D

know your old dial in a Sahara sandstorm.

PADDY. Well, in sowl, you've the advantage of me; for, asleep or awake, I've never seen you before.

O'CAHAN. Nonsense, Paddy. You know him all right. Mrs. Scally's brother — Professor Tim.

PADDY. Ah, surely to God! It's Tim of the hazel rod. [Shaking hands] And how's every square inch of you, Professor?

PROFESSOR. Begum, Paddy, I'm not as robust as I was. The years are not getting any fewer. And I've been travelling a deal lately. I'm tired.

PADDY. You want a month on the grass with the shoes off.

PROFESSOR. That's just the cure, Paddy. A grass holiday.

PADDY. Well, Professor, I'm glad to see you. Keep a good spirit. Plenty of good mate and drink and the pure air'll soon bring you into condition.

PROFESSOR. But where am I to get all that, Paddy? The Scallys don't want me. My own sister pushed me out of doors.

PADDY. And for a man that has travelled the world — what did you expect?

PROFESSOR. I didn't expect much, Paddy. But I didn't reckon on downright bad treatment.

PADDY. Well, that was your mistake, Professor. For when a man is down as far as he can get, his own relations give him the last kick. [Gives him a coin.] There's a couple of bob, Tim. I wish 'twas more. But there's a basket of corn-beef, cakes, and porter in the hall. Let you help yourself.

PROFESSOR [takes the money]. Thanks, Paddy. You're a good Irishman.

PADDY. Yerra, nonsense! Sure an ould timer's an ould timer, whether he's down or up.

O'CAHAN. The Professor wants you to see about his valise, Paddy.

PADDY. With pleasure.

PROFESSOR. I seem to've dropped it somewhere, Paddy. It's either at Ballykennedy station or London.

PADDY. I'll try Ballykennedy first.

PROFESSOR. My goodness, yes: you'd get lost in London.

O'CAHAN. You can go after a bit, Paddy. . . . Come on, Professor.

MOLL. Are you not looking at my new dress, master.

O'CAHAN. I've been looking at nothing else, Moll. You're like an oil painting. [*To* PADDY] In you, Paddy, the French lost a great milliner.

PROFESSOR. Begum, Moll, I've travelled seven times round the world and never seen a more devastating colour scheme. You're like a bird of paradise.

MOLL. I wouldn't like to be too peacockish.

PROFESSOR. You're more, I think, of a macaw. [*He and* O'CAHAN *go out.*]

PADDY. So that's the end of Tim. That man's as far down as he can get by land. And I mind him a nice young fella, as full o' tricks as a monkey.

MOLL. He's an eye for a well-dressed woman anyway. Seven times round the world and never seen the likes of it. I must take great care of it, Paddy. [*Takes hat off.*] I'll keep the dress on till after the auction.

PADDY [*takes out a trotting collar and tie*]. Listen to

me, Moll Flanagan, and not a word of this to the boss. . . .

MOLL. Lord save us, Paddy, you look very serious. You're not going to mention marriage. . . .

PADDY. I've no intention of marriage. I've trouble enough without marrying more.

MOLL. That's pure imperence.

PADDY. Listen to what I'm saying. Isn't there a black coat and hat of the ould master's upstairs?

MOLL. There's a full black suit, not a pin the worse, and a beautiful hat.

PADDY. Well, take and brush them well and slip them round to the stable. And don't let a living sowl see you. I'm going to dress up like a country squire and make the Kilroys pay for Rush Hill.

MOLL. My darlin' Paddy! Lord, but that's a noble trick. . . . I'll brush them up and take them round under my apron.

PADDY. By my sowl, if we've to get out cheap, the Kilroys'll have to come in dear. I'll salt it on them to the bone. . . .

MOLL. Hide the collar and tie. . . . I hear someone coming in.

PEGGY *comes in.*

PEGGY. Where is Mr. O'Cahan?

MOLL. In the kitchen, honey.

PEGGY. Anyone with him?

MOLL. The Professor of Theeology——

PADDY. Mind your tongue, Moll.

PEGGY. It's all right, Paddy. Moll wouldn't sting me.

MOLL. God knows I wouldn't. I love and respect the ground you walk on.

PEGGY. Tell Mr. O'Cahan to come here, Moll. You needn't say who wants him.

MOLL. Not a word, dear. [*At the door*] Do you like my new dress, Miss Peggy?

PEGGY. Very much indeed, Moll. Your health to wear it.

MOLL. It's a thought too stylish for the likes of me, but it's a good fault. The hat to match it is in the bag. Show it to her, Paddy. [*Goes out.*]

PADDY. Are you going to marry him, Peggy?

PEGGY. I'm afraid not, Paddy. Too many things have gone against us.

PADDY. That's the very time to lay your cheek to the mane and ride for your life . . . when the race is all but lost.

PEGGY. It's not so easy, Paddy.

PADDY. You'll never find a mate like Hugh O'Cahan.

PEGGY. I know it.

PADDY. There's only one Hugh O'Cahan born in every hundred years. Such an archangel on a horse! Lord, 'twas a pome to see him taking the stone wall. And the double-bank — touching it as light as a thistledown.

PEGGY. I know, Paddy. I know.

PADDY. Says the white-haired judge, and he tucking the red roseatte in the bridle, " I've never in the coorse of a long life," says he, " beheld such classical leppin'. Your horse can jump like a flea." That was a day!

PEGGY. I know, Paddy. I was there.

PADDY. Did I ever tell you the story about the brown horse, Havoc, the time he pulled O'Cahan out of the saddle and up on his neck?

PEGGY. You did, Paddy . . . several times. Now, you'll excuse me, Paddy. I want a few private words with Hugh.

PADDY. Certainly. I'll pull out the minute he comes in. . . . But do what I tell you now. Go with him wherever he goes. Put your money on O'Cahan. He's only five-and-twenty. At thirty he'll be one of the great men of the world. [*He dries the perspiration off his face.*]

PEGGY. He's already a three-quarter vet. Why doesn't he finish?

PADDY. Ay — to vet Ford cars. . . . It's disgusting! The blight is upon us, Peggy. The horse is going, the O'Cahans are going, and the Paddy Kinneys are doomed. . . .

PEGGY. I hear him coming, Paddy.

PADDY. All right, I'm going. But don't forget Paddy Kinney's warning, or you'll never know happiness again. Without O'Cahan by your side you won't know the summer from the winter but by the leaves on the bushes. . . .

O'CAHAN *comes in, looking displeased.* PADDY *goes out, doleful.*

PEGGY. I see you're angry, Hugh. But mother sent me after Uncle Tim.

O'CAHAN. I'm not angry; I'm ashamed of this place.

PEGGY. I'm not looking at the place. Is uncle in the kitchen?

O'CAHAN. Yes.

PEGGY. Will you tell him to go home? Mother wants him back.

O'CAHAN. I'm not holding him, but I won't ask

him to go. That would be breaking an old custom in this house.

PEGGY. Will you let me see him?

O'CAHAN. I think he's coming in. . . . [*Shouts*] Come in, Professor.

PEGGY. Hugh, don't call him Professor. It hurts.

PROFESSOR *comes in eating biscuits and cheese.*

PROFESSOR. Hullo, pretty Peggy. Have you tracked me down already?

O'CAHAN. I'll leave you——

PEGGY. You needn't, Hugh. I only want Uncle Tim to come home.

PROFESSOR. Want the luxury of throwing me out again?

PEGGY. I didn't throw you out.

PROFESSOR. Your mother did.

PEGGY. Well, she wants you back. She sent me to fetch you. The stationmaster has sent out your valise.

PROFESSOR. Your mother must think it contains something valuable. [*Chuckles.*] Begum, she's mistaken. The contents are a few old clothes and a hazel rod — the symbol of my profession.

PEGGY. Hugh, please tell him to come home.

O'CAHAN. He can suit himself, Peggy. He knows the position of affairs here.

PROFESSOR. We're going to have an auction here. Begum, I must stay and see a bit of Irish life.

PADDY *comes to the door.*

PADDY. There's a railway porter here with an ould port-mantle. He wants a tip.

PROFESSOR. Begum, Paddy, you've got a sense of

humour. [*Going.*] I thought I'd dropped it in London. [*He and* PADDY *go.*]

PEGGY. Are the Kilroys here?

O'CAHAN. Yes . . . hovering around like jackals.

PEGGY. They're going to buy Rush Hill for Joseph and me.

O'CAHAN. So I understand.

PEGGY. And you don't mind?

O'CAHAN. Supposing I did mind — would that alter it?

PEGGY. You never know. Marrying Joseph is one thing, but coming to live here is another.

O'CAHAN. If you can do the one you can do both.

PEGGY. I may do neither. What time are you leaving here to-night?

O'CAHAN. Whatever time the last train goes. Seven o'clock, I think.

PEGGY. I'm going to ask you one question: how much money have you?

O'CAHAN. I got two hundred pounds for Havoc. I've got that, but I've to pay a colt out of it. Forty pounds.

PEGGY [*takes out packet*]. These presents would make two hundred more. If you don't sell them, I will.

O'CAHAN. Suit yourself.

PEGGY. Will you call at our house before you go?

O'CAHAN. What's the idea?

PEGGY. It's my own idea. Will you call?

O'CAHAN. Some new notion. Yes, I'll look in.

PEGGY. Thanks. [*Puts packet in her pocket.*] I'll go now and get Uncle Tim out of here. . . .

PROFESSOR *comes in with an old valise plastered with innumerable labels.*

PROFESSOR. Begum, this old valise and me have seen some ups and downs. [*Lays it on a chair and fumbles for the key.*] I've dropped it in Paris and picked it up in Honolulu. . . .

PEGGY. Aren't you coming home, uncle?

PROFESSOR. It's been stolen in London and restored to me in Japan. [*He opens it.*] A man might as well try to lose his third wife.

PEGGY. Aren't you coming with me, uncle?

PROFESSOR [*takes out a hazel rod*]. I'm going to do a little professional work. I've an idea this house is built on a spring. [*He starts prospecting for water.*]

PEGGY. Uncle Tim!

O'CAHAN. Leave him alone, Peggy. It's interesting.

PROFESSOR. There's water here, somewhere. [*The rod vibrates.*] Wo, gal! [*The rod dips.*] Gum, this is it. [*The rod twists violently out of his hand.*] Yes. Three springs converge at a point fifty feet deep.

O'CAHAN. It must be a lake.

PROFESSOR. No, no! A lake has no life. It's dead. A spring has a pulse and lives. I can hear a spring breathing.

PEGGY. Now, uncle, aren't you coming? You've done very well, you've shown us up.

O'CAHAN. Yes, Tim, you'd better go home with your niece. I'll see you again before I leave.

PROFESSOR. Right, boss. Whatever you say is an order. [*He puts the rod in the valise and is going out with* PEGGY.]

O'CAHAN. If you leave your valise in the hall, I'll send Paddy over with it.

PEGGY. Thanks, Hugh. [*She and* PROFESSOR *go out.*]

o'CAHAN [*calls*]. Paddy!

MOLL [*off*]. Paddy's in the stable, master. [*She comes in.*] Is it anything very urgent?

o'CAHAN. Tell him to take that valise over to Scally's.

MOLL. I'll do that. [*Sighs.*] Och, hum! I hate to break the news, master, but the auctioneer's coming.

o'CAHAN. I heard the car, Moll. The sooner it's over the better. [*Looks out.*] It's going to rain.

MOLL. I hope it rains in oceans and drowns the grabbers. [*She gets a chair and turns the uncle's portrait face to the wall.*] No use letting him see the end of it.

o'CAHAN. Not a bit, Moll. It wouldn't do him — or us — any good.

As MOLL *goes out* ALLISON *comes in. He has an attaché case.*

ALLISON. Good morning, Mr. O'Cahan. You'll hardly believe it — I'd rather go a thousand miles than do this job.

o'CAHAN. I don't believe a word of it, Sam. But I understand — you have to say something. Even the undertaker has to say something.

ALLISON. Will you believe this: I take no pleasure in selling you up.

o'CAHAN. I accept that. And you can believe this: since it has to be sold I'd rather see you here than anyone else.

ALLISON. Thank you. I know it. Now, James Kilroy is going to buy it.

o'CAHAN. So I understand.

ALLISON. Have you anyone here to run it up on him?

o'CAHAN. No. I don't believe in doing dirty work for the bank.

ALLISON. Paddy Kinney has destroyed all chance of a normal sale. He made a house-to-house canvass and got the people to boycott the auction.

o'CAHAN. If he did I knew nothing about it. But it's like a thing Paddy would do.

ALLISON. I'm going to tell you a secret, Hugh. The bank's reserve price is three thousand pounds. If it doesn't make that at the auction it won't be sold.

o'CAHAN. It won't make it.

ALLISON. Then Kilroy'll have a private deal with the bank. You see? You ought to've had someone here to run it up.

o'CAHAN. I personally don't care whether it makes three thousand pounds or three shillings. Sale or no sale, I'm clearing out to-night.

ALLISON. Oh, that's different.

KILROY, JOSEPH, *and* JOHN SCALLY *come in.*

KILROY. I hope we're not intruding. It's going to rain.

o'CAHAN. This is an auction. You're welcome. [*He stands over at the sideboard.*]

KILROY. You're not going to've a big crowd, Mr. Allison.

ALLISON. Evidently not.

o'CAHAN. The number of local grabbers is smaller than you thought.

KILROY. I don't like the way you put that, sir!

o'CAHAN. That's exactly why I put it that way.

KILROY [*hotly*]. Do you call me a grabber, sir?

o'CAHAN. Now, don't lose your head. This isn't

a meeting of the Rural Council.

KILROY. By heavens, O'Cahan, you and your uncle always treated me like dirt!

O'CAHAN. We always treated a man as we found him.

KILROY. Well, it's my turn now. I'm here to buy Rush Hill for my son Joseph. . . . Now, Allison, read the terms. It's after eleven o'clock.

PADDY *comes in, dressed like a man of means.*

PADDY. Is the sile ovah?

ALLISON. No, sir, it's not on yet.

PADDY. Owh, that's lucky.

KILROY. Read the terms, Mr. Allison.

ALLISON. Not in here. I'll go out to the front steps.

KILROY. Well, come on. I don't care where you read them. [*He and* JOSEPH, PADDY, JOHN, *and* ALLISON *go out.*]

O'CAHAN [*stands listening*]. Poor Kinney! [*Smiles.*] Sile ovah. . . . Paddy's as much a part of Rush Hill as the O'Cahans.

MRS. SCALLY *comes in.*

MRS. SCALLY. Where is my daughter Peggy?

O'CAHAN. At the moment I don't know.

MRS. SCALLY. She came over here half an hour ago. Where is she, sir?

O'CAHAN. Not here. And you needn't take up that attitude with me. I'm neither your husband nor one of your offspring.

MRS. SCALLY. Thank my God you're nothing to me!

O'CAHAN. Amen. One couldn't be too grateful.

MRS. SCALLY. You've lost everything but your brazen cheek.

O'CAHAN. You haven't lost yours anyway.

MRS. SCALLY. When I'm here I'll give you a bit of my mind. You're a disgrace to the parish. A walking disgrace.

O'CAHAN. I never contradict people like you.

MRS. SCALLY. Because you can't. The proof is here to be seen: desolation everywhere. [*Looks round room.*] Yes: the tree is known by its fruit.

O'CAHAN. In Ireland a man is better known by the number of people who stay away from his auction.

MRS. SCALLY. The condition of this room tells a long story. . . .

O'CAHAN. I'm sorry you weren't here a little sooner. The eminent Professor was prospecting for water.

MRS. SCALLY. You're a likely one to be scoffing——

O'CAHAN. I'm not scoffing. I think Professor Tim a very interesting man.

MRS. SCALLY. You no doubt have a lot in common.

O'CAHAN. Far more than you think. I could never have too much of Tim, or too little of you. [*Yawns.*] Excuse me.

MRS. SCALLY. I ask you again, where is Peggy?

O'CAHAN. She and the Professor left here to go home.

MRS. SCALLY. Did they go the back way?

O'CAHAN. They must have, if you didn't meet them.

MRS. SCALLY. What's the valise doing in the hall?

O'CAHAN. It's waiting there for Paddy Kinney to carry it across. If you want it you can have it.

MRS. SCALLY. I don't want it. I'll stay here and see the auction.

O'CAHAN. You're very welcome. Will you sit down?

MRS. SCALLY. No, I'll just look about me.

ALLISON *in the doorway.*

ALLISON. Mr. O'Cahan, could I've something to stand up on? It's going to be a downpour. . . .

O'CAHAN. Why not come in here? I haven't the smallest objection.

MRS. SCALLY. Come in, Mr. Allison. Come in, Mr. Kilroy.

ALLISON, KILROY, JOSEPH, JOHN, *and* PADDY *come in.*

ALLISON [*mounting a chair*]. We may as well make a start. . . .

MRS. SCALLY. Good gracious, is this all the people?

ALLISON. I'm sorry to say it is, madam. The sale has been boycotted.

MRS. SCALLY. Oh, well, it'll go all the cheaper.

ALLISON [*takes out hammer*]. Gentlemen, you've heard the terms of sale. I've also told you that the bank has fixed a reserve price below which Rush Hill can't be sold to-day. Now, I'll take offers.

MRS. SCALLY. Come, John. Bid up.

JOHN [*dourly*]. Let somebody else start it. I hate these auction-outs.

MOLL *appears in the doorway.*

MOLL. Here's the great Professor Tim . . . looking for his sister Bridget Scally.

KILROY. Good, good! Bring in the Professor.

This is most fortunate. . . .

MRS. SCALLY [*reeling towards door*]. No, no, no! Don't let him in here.

MOLL [*pushing her back*]. Stay in there, Vanity Fair! till the hand of God falls on you in public. [*Shouts.*] Come in, Professor! Come in. Your sister Bridget's just dying to meet you.

PROFESSOR *staggers in.* KILROY *gasps.*

PROFESSOR. Hullo, all. Am I in time? Begum, it's a very small auction.

KILROY. Who in the devil's name is this?

MRS. SCALLY. Mr. Kilroy, this is my brother. He gave us to understand he was a professor. And there he is — a disgrace. And Hugh O'Cahan has made the most of him.

KILROY. I see now. This has all been staged for the auction. But it won't work.

MRS. SCALLY. That's the style, James. That's common sense. This tramp's visit needn't interfere with our plans. He'll go away to-night . . . he can go with O'Cahan.

PROFESSOR. I'll go when I'm ready. [*To* ALLISON] Go on, mister. Open the bazaar. It's over twenty years since I attended an Irish auction.

KILROY. Go ahead, Allison. Five hundred pounds.

ALLISON. I won't accept that bid.

PADDY. Fifteen 'undred.

MOLL. Hurrah!

ALLISON. That's better. I'm offered fifteen hundred pounds.

PROFESSOR. Two thousand. It's worth that if it's worth a penny.

MRS. SCALLY. Mr. Allison, this man hasn't a white

sixpence. I'll have to give him a few shillings to take him away.

PADDY. Twenty-two 'undred.

ALLISON. Steady now, gentlemen. I'm bid twenty-two hundred pounds.

JOSEPH [*wildly*]. Twenty-two-fifty!

KILROY. Easy now, Joseph. Don't get excited. [*He drags* JOSEPH *away*.]

PADDY. Twenty-four 'undred.

PROFESSOR. Twenty-five hundred.

PADDY. Twenty-six.

PROFESSOR. Twenty-seven.

PADDY. Twenty-nine.

PROFESSOR [*to* PADDY]. Begum, you're a crafty gentleman. You want it knocked down to me at three thousand.

KILROY [*loudly*]. This is a put-up job! The whole thing — Professor and all — is a piece of O'Cahan's twisting. . . .

O'CAHAN [*crossing to him*]. Say that again.

JOSEPH [*gets behind* KILROY]. Now, father — into him!

KILROY [*afraid*]. Didn't you call me a grabber?

O'CAHAN. And what are you? Haven't you got a home of your own?

JOSEPH. Intil him, father!

O'CAHAN. Listen to me, Kilroy. I've been taught in good company to take what comes; to win or lose all like a sportsman. But I allow no white man to call me a twister. If you open your mouth to me again, you and your clown of a son'll leave this room feet first. [*Returns to his place*.]

JOSEPH [*shivering*]. Intil him, father. He struck me with a whip.

PROFESSOR. My advice to you, young man, is to keep quiet. Your father's too old, and you're too young; and I've grave doubts as to your courage.

ALLISON. I'm selling this farm. You can exchange compliments later. [*To* PADDY] Your last bid is twenty-nine hundred pounds.

PADDY. Yes. Knock it dahn.

ALLISON. I'm offered two thousand, nine hundred pounds, by a stranger who has evidently come to buy Rush Hill and who has no quarrel with anyone. Any advance?

PROFESSOR. Another fifty pounds. Keep the ball rolling.

MRS. SCALLY [*shrieks*]. Don't take his bid! The man couldn't buy a box of matches. . . . James Kilroy, a word with you and Joseph. [*They go to the window and confer in whispers.*]

PROFESSOR. Did you take my bid, mister?

ALLISON. No, sir. I don't want to hear from you again. If you've the money to buy Rush Hill you should invest in a cake of soap. . . .

PROFESSOR. Mister, you've got no more brains than the hammer in your hand.

The KILROYS *and* MRS. SCALLY *return to the ring.*

ALLISON. Well, Mr. Kilroy: are you going to give me another bid?

JOSEPH. Gwon, father.

KILROY [*after a glance at* PADDY). Three thousand pounds——

PADDY. Thirty-one 'undred.

KILROY [*losing his head*]. Thirty-two hundred——

PADDY. Thirty-three 'undred——

KILROY [*dancing*]. Thirty-four——

E

PADDY. Thirty-four-fifty——

KILROY. Thirty-five hundred!

PADDY [*turns away*]. I'm through.

KILROY [*grabbing hold of him*]. Don't go away!
Stand your ground like a man. . . .

PADDY [*freeing himself*]. Mind your own business.
I'm through.

ALLISON. At three thousand, five hundred pounds
. . . going . . . going——

KILROY. Wait, Allison! [*Looks wildly at* PADDY.]
Come on, man.   Give it another bid.

PADDY. No more.   I'm through.   [*Exit, followed
by* MOLL.]

ALLISON. If no advance, at three thousand, five
hundred . . . going . . . going . . . gone.   Mr.
James J. Kilroy's the buyer.

JOSEPH. Hurray for my father!   He can buy
Rush Hill.   And I can marry Peggy Scally.   [*He
runs out.*]

KILROY [*sighs*]. I'm ruined!

ALLISON [*getting down*]. Nonsense.   It's worth
five thousand pounds.   [*Takes out document.*]   Sign
this, James.

KILROY. I'll sign nothing here.   I'll sign at the
bank.   I'm going straight to the bank.

ALLISON. I'm the auctioneer.   As agent for buyer
and seller I can sign for both.   [*He writes* KILROY's
name.]

PROFESSOR. That's right, Allison.   Don't let the
big codfish escape.

KILROY [*pulling himself together*]. James J. Kilroy,
R.D.C., never hedged in a deal yet.   I wanted Rush
Hill at less money, but it's worth all it cost.   Give
me that pen, Allison.   I'll sign.

ALLISON. It's all right, James; I signed your name. You can meet me at the bank at two o'clock.

KILROY. I'll be there.

ALLISON. Good-bye, Mr. O'Cahan. Thank you for treating us so well.

O'CAHAN. Don't mention it, Sam.

ALLISON *goes out.*]

PROFESSOR. Kilroy, we made you pay through the nose for it.

KILROY. Mrs. Scally, if you've this man about the house to-night, I needn't bring Mrs. Kilroy.

MRS. SCALLY. You leave that to me, James. Bring your wife over at six o'clock as we arranged.

KILROY. Well, I will. [*He goes.*]

MRS. SCALLY. John, who was that strange man that run up the price?

JOHN. I neither know nor care!

PADDY *comes in, in his old clothes.*

PADDY. The strange man, is it? I can tell you who he was. He was a man the bank sent out to sweeten it. And I can tell you more. Kilroy's the buyer, but he'll have the devil of a time getting bail.

JOHN. By hokey, that's news!

MRS. SCALLY. Silence, John. Would you heed a drunken horse-boy? [*To* PROFESSOR] Tim, dear, come with me. You need a good rest. You're tired.

PROFESSOR. Stand back, Bridget. I don't want a rest — closed in the barn. [*Loudly*] My valise! Where's my valise?

MRS. SCALLY. Where are you going?

PROFESSOR. I'm for off. Important engagement in London.

MRS. SCALLY. That's a good man. Keep your appointment, or I'll put you where you won't upset my plans for at least a week. [*To* JOHN] Is James Kilroy away?

JOHN. No, he's out there at the front.

MRS. SCALLY. Go and tell him I want him. Quick now!

JOHN. Yah! [*Goes out.*]

PROFESSOR. My valise!

MOLL *comes in with valise.*

MOLL. Here it is, Professor. I suppose all your theeology tools are in it. [*Puts it down beside him.*]

PROFESSOR. Good-bye, O'Cahan. Thanks for the bread and cheese. That's more than I've to thank my sister for.

O'CAHAN. Don't mention it, my friend. [*Gives him money.*] Sorry I'm leaving here myself, or you could have lain around and had a good rest.

PROFESSOR [*salutes*]. You're a chip of the old block. In rain or shine, the O'Cahans were fine men. [*To* PADDY] Good-bye, Paddy Kinney. Thanks for the two shillings——

MRS. SCALLY. Lord above! did you take money from Paddy Kinney?

PROFESSOR. I did, and was very glad to get it. Good-bye, Paddy.

PADDY. Good-bye, Tim. May we all see better days.

PROFESSOR. Adieu, Moll Flanagan. Don't sit on a barrel of gunpowder with that dress.

MOLL. Good-bye, ye ould wreck ye! Yourself and that portmantual should be taken out to the bog and buried in it.

PROFESSOR. A long rest in an Irish bog would suit me well.   I'm so tired.

KILROY *and* JOHN *come in.*

MRS. SCALLY. James Kilroy, will you drive my brother to the station?   He wants to catch the first train. . . .

KILROY. I'd drive him to the very devil!   [*To* PROFESSOR] Where are you going?

PROFESSOR. Important engagement in London.

KILROY. Gimme that ould bag!   And come with me.   [*Takes valise.*]   It won't be my fault if you miss the train.   [*He goes out.*]

PROFESSOR. My sister, I won't bid you good-bye. You treated me like a yellow dog.   [*To* JOHN] Good-bye, Johnny.   I don't blame you at all. You're only a scarecrow on your own farm.   A domestic serf.

JOHN. I've no money, Tim, or I'd give you some.

PROFESSOR. It's all right, Johnny.   I understand your financial status.   Your wife carries the purse in her breeches pocket.   [*He goes out.*]

MRS. SCALLY. Oh, thank my God to be rid of that visitation!

PADDY. Don't have your thanks-givin' service too soon, ma'am.   He might come back.

MRS. SCALLY. Come on, John.   We'll watch till they put him in the trap.   [*She and* JOHN *go out.*]

MOLL [*sighs*]. Och, hum!   [*She tears down the curtain.*]

PADDY. Didn't I give the mastiff Kilroy a good run for his money, boss?

O'CAHAN. Very good, Paddy.   [*He takes down the uncle's portrait, then points to the sideboard.*]   Paddy, take those cups and things in to O'Hanlon, the vet, and tell him to keep them for me till I send for them. . . . And you and Moll can carry away as much of the other stuff as you like. I'm leaving Rush Hill to-night.

O'CAHAN *goes out.* PADDY *and* MOLL *exchange a long look, then turn back and weep quietly.*

Curtain

ACT III

The same as in Act I. The PROFESSOR *has returned from town. He is half asleep in a chair at the table. His valise is lying on the floor.*

PEGGY *comes in cautiously from the room. She has a hat and coat and small suitcase, which she hides in the lower part of the cupboard.*

PEGGY [*regarding* PROFESSOR]. Wake up, uncle. [*No response.*] Gracious, wasn't mother and the Kilroys foolish to think you'd go away. . . . Important engagement in London.

PROFESSOR [*looks up vacantly and scratches his head*]. I wonder to Gawd where I'm now! Paris or London. . . .

PEGGY. You're all right, uncle. You're at home in Ireland.

PROFESSOR [*parrot-like*]. Pritty Peggy, pritty Peggy . . . lent me three pounds at five per cent. . . . Rich or poor, you're my uncle Peggy. . . . Full or empty, welcome home. . . . Order, order! [*Sleeps.*]

PEGGY. It's perfectly hopeless. [*Goes out, back.*]

PROFESSOR [*sits up again*]. Whisht, Kelly! By some mysterious dispensation of Providence you can sing none. Let me try it. [*Sings:*]

" I'm a daughter of Daniel O'Connell,
    From England last week I sailed o'er;
    The people to me are all strangers,
    I don't know my friends from my foes."

[*Scratching his head*] If a man doesn't know his friends from his foes, he has only to come home broke. [*Sleeps.*]

JOHN *comes in at the back. He is coatless and has the salley switch in his hand.*

JOHN. Are you sleeping, Tim? [*No answer.*] Waken up, man! I'm going to cart you over to the other farm. . . .

PROFESSOR. Whisht, Kelly! You're murdering it. Let me at it. [*Sings:*]

" I must confess I am content, no more I wish to
    roam,
  So steer my barque for Erin's Isle, for Erin is
    my home."

Kelly, I'm home-sick. I'll go home to-morrow — should I've to walk it.

JOHN. Poor fellow!

MRS. SCALLY *comes in from the room. She has her hair done and wears a grand frock and a conspicuous watch-chain.*

MRS. SCALLY. Give him a shake, man! Don't be so gentle with him.

JOHN. I could never cart this man across, Bridget, in such a condition. He's like a lump of wet putty.

MRS. SCALLY. You'll take him over and close him in the barn, and he'll stay there till I give the order to release him. I'll not have my plans upset by a wandering vagabond. [*She grabs the switch from* JOHN *and hits the* PROFESSOR *a lick.*] Waken up! or I'll lift the bark off you. [*It has no effect.*]

JOHN. See that now, Bridget. He's paralysed.

MRS. SCALLY. And them Kilroys coming in a few minutes!

JOHN. If we could get him upstairs, and let him lie in the back room.

MRS. SCALLY [*explodes and batters* PROFESSOR]. Get up! Rise! Wake up — or I'll finish you!

JOHN [*takes switch away from her*]. Don't do that, woman! Don't hammer the unfortunate.

PROFESSOR [*awake*]. What's the row?

MRS. SCALLY. Get up!

PROFESSOR. Where am I? Who struck me with the marlinspike?

MRS. SCALLY. I did. Get up.

PROFESSOR [*yawns*]. I'm tired.

MRS. SCALLY. Well, there's a room upstairs. Go up and lie down. John'll help you up.

PROFESSOR. What time is it?

MRS. SCALLY. It's bedtime.

JOHN. Ah no, Bridget, it's not six o'clock.

MRS. SCALLY [*to* JOHN]. Fat head!

PROFESSOR [*blinking*]. I'm not going to bed at six o'clock, like in a reformatory. I want a drink. . . .

MRS. SCALLY. You'll get no drink here, not a spark.

PROFESSOR. My valise! Where's my valise?

MRS. SCALLY. It's here. [*To* JOHN] Take it up to the back room. Quick now!

JOHN *goes out with valise.*

PROFESSOR. Come back here, Johnny. Come back, you little cutworm. [*Draws knife.*] Begum, I'll teach you crofters manners. [*Goes out after* JOHN.]

MRS. SCALLY. Oh, sweet bad luck to you! And

the same to big, windy Kilroy, for leaving you on the platform instead of flinging you into the train.

PEGGY *comes in.*

PEGGY. What's wrong, mother?

MRS. SCALLY. What's not wrong?

PEGGY. Where's Uncle Tim?

MRS. SCALLY. The last I saw of him he was chasing your father upstairs with a knife. This house is going straight to the devil.

PEGGY. He might hurt father.

MRS. SCALLY. He hasn't the least intention of hurting father. He knows soft John too well for that.

PEGGY. There's always something wrong in this house.

MRS. SCALLY. Yes, and there's something wrong with you too. You've been flitting about all afternoon like a ghost. I've eyes in my head.

PEGGY. Mother, you do have some queer notions. You'd think I was only sixteen.

MRS. SCALLY. Your age has nothing whatever to do with it. You're under my care till Joseph Kilroy takes you off my hand, then you'll be your own mistress.

PEGGY. You're making a sermon out of nothing.

MRS. SCALLY. Well, I'll cut my sermon short. You'll marry Joseph Kilroy immediately. His mother'll be here in a few minutes and I'll make my own arrangements. Go now and close the parlour windows and have everything ready for tea. . . .

JOHN *comes in shaking his head.*

JOHN. That's a case! He lay down on the parlour floor and fell asleep.

MRS. SCALLY [*shrieks*]. Why did you let him in there! Go at once and drag him out. Don't you know the Kilroys have to sit in there. Drag him out, I say.

JOHN. By hokey, I'll do nothing of the kind. He's that long seafaring knife in his hand, and vows he'll give somebody the length of it. I'll not face him anyway.

MRS. SCALLY. You'll not face him! [*Blazing*] But I'll face him! [*Goes to the room.*]

JOHN. Your mother's getting very hard to live with, Peggy. She's out of one tantrum into another the whole year round. I've made myself an old man trying to humour that woman and keep peace in the house, but it's going to beat me in the end.

Noise from MRS. SCALLY *and* PROFESSOR *in the room.*

PEGGY. Listen, father. She's giving him a great tongue trashing.

JOHN. She won't shift him. You might as well try to draw the badger.

PEGGY. I thought you were going to take him over to the other farm.

JOHN. The man's not able to go anywhere. He wants about a month's sleep. God knows when that man had a dacent sleep. Maybe not for years.

PEGGY. Well, it's a pity. The Kilroys are coming and we can't take them to the room.

JOHN. What's the matter with this kitchen?

PEGGY. Not a thing, father. But Mrs. Kilroy's coming.

JOHN. And who's Mrs. Kilroy? Is she any better than the rest of us?

PEGGY. Not a bit. But she thinks she is.

JOHN. The priest sits in this kitchen. If it's good enough for him it's good enough for Mrs. Kilroy. I'm fair sick of vanity.

PEGGY. Just a word, father, before they come in. Don't you sign any papers for James Kilroy. Hugh O'Cahan says they've nothing.

JOHN. Do you think I don't know what Kilroy's here for? And what all the match-making's about? Ho, the very best. His ill-bred son wants a settlement and there's nothing to settle him with. . . .

PEGGY. They shan't settle him with me.

JOHN. You're right, Peggy. If I was a nice educated girl like you I'd put a shirt on Hugh O'Cahan. He's a man with all his faults; the other's a prig with all his virtues.

PEGGY. Father, I never thought you could size up people so well.

JOHN. Oh, I'm not as soft as I let on, Peggy. By minding my own business I'm a strong farmer. Kilroy, by minding other people's business, is a weak one. He'd ruin me now like himself, but I won't let him.

PEGGY. Mother'll be wild if you don't sign.

JOHN. I know, Peggy: it means civil war. But I'm prepared for war. Your mother treated me very shabby this day. It was " Silence, John! " every time I opened my mouth. Your Uncle Tim said I was only a scarecrow on my own farm, and he wasn't far wrong. But, by God, the scarecrow's tired of his job!

MRS. SCALLY *comes in, baffled and angry.*

MRS. SCALLY. Have you pair been tittlin' here ever since!

JOHN. We were waiting for you, Bridget, to bring out the invader.

MRS. SCALLY. But you couldn't come and give me a hand!

JOHN. I knew if you couldn't shift him yourself, nothing could shift him.

MRS. SCALLY [to PEGGY]. You didn't think it worth while to come!

PEGGY. I was afraid, mother. He was ravelling in his sleep. You never know what he'd do.

MRS. SCALLY. Well, put on your apron and lay the table. We'll have to entertain the Kilroys in here.

PEGGY. All right, mother. [Gets tablecloth.]

MRS. SCALLY [to JOHN]. Go you and leave your cowstick outside and put something clean on your neck. You'll be sitting at the table with Mrs. Kilroy.

JOHN. That's a great honour. Peggy, is there a rag of a collar about the house?

PEGGY. Your collar and tie are here. [Gets them from a drawer.]

JOHN. Put them on me, Peggy, like a good girl. My hands is dirty.

MRS. SCALLY. And so is your face! Go out and wash your face and hands at the pump.

JOHN. I'll attend to all that in a minute, Bridget.

PEGGY puts collar and tie on JOHN. MRS. SCALLY goes to the room and returns with a grand red chair.

MRS. SCALLY. If I'd a man like a man, and not a jinny, he'd soon clear the room! [Goes out for another chair.]

JOHN. Peggy, she's working herself up into a serious pucker.

PEGGY. Never mind, father.

JOHN. I'm as much to blame as she is. I let her tramp over me at the start. Before you childer grew up I was servant girl and all here.

MRS. SCALLY *comes in with another chair.*

MRS. SCALLY. If my three sons were here they'd soon clear the room! [*Goes out for a plant.*]

JOHN. You'd think they weren't my sons too. . . . If ever you marry, Peggy, never treat your man like that.

PEGGY. Now, now, father: don't get vexed with her. After all, she's a good mother, and she improved you.

JOHN. She improved me, but at a terrible price.

MRS. SCALLY *comes in with a geranium in a pot.*

MRS. SCALLY. If these strangers weren't coming, I'd give you pair a bit of my mind. [*Staring at them*] Are you going to stand there thumbing and fiddling till they walk in?

JOHN. Hurry up, Peggy.

PEGGY. There you are, father.

JOHN. I'll go now and have a nice wash at the pump. [*Goes out.*]

MRS. SCALLY. Get the tablecloth.

PEGGY [*gets cloth*]. Will you just give them tea in their hands?

MRS. SCALLY. I'll see when the time comes. Straighten the cloth.

PEGGY *spreads the cloth and* MRS. SCALLY *puts the geranium in the centre.*

PEGGY [*going to cupboard*]. I'll get out the cups. . . .

MRS. SCALLY. Never mind the cups. I'll get them out myself. Put on your apron.

PEGGY *gets an apron and watches* MRS. SCALLY *nervously. She opens cupboard and takes out tea-things. Then she peers into the lower part and drags out* PEGGY's *hat, coat, and suitcase.*

PEGGY. O-h!

MRS. SCALLY [*very calm*]. What are these things doing here?

PEGGY [*stiffly*]. I don't know.

MRS. SCALLY. When did you put them in there?

PEGGY. I don't know.

MRS. SCALLY. Perhaps they don't belong to you?

PEGGY. I don't know.

MRS. SCALLY. Since you don't appear to know anything, I must find out for myself. [*Tries to open suitcase.*] Where's the key of this bag?

PEGGY. I don't know.

MRS. SCALLY [*flies into a temper and tries to smash it*]. I'll smash more than the bag before I've finished! I'll have no runaway matches in my house. . . .

JOHN *hurries in, drying his face on an old towel.*

JOHN. Here they come, Bridget! The Royal Procession. James and the wife and Joseph.

MRS. SCALLY. Go you and put on your hat and coat and meet them and put in the horse and throw that old towel out of your hand!

JOHN. By hokey, that's a fine string of orders. [*Sees suitcase.*] What's this . . .?

MRS. SCALLY. Step on and do what you're told!

JOHN. Holy tattler! [*Going.*] As Tim says, it's like a house of correction. [*Goes out.*]

PEGGY. Father's getting pretty sick of all this stupid badgering. And so am I. It makes life a burden.

MRS. SCALLY. If these strangers weren't coming in I'd give you and your father a lesson. . . .

PROFESSOR *staggers in.*

PROFESSOR. A drink of water, please.

MRS. SCALLY. Oooooooh!

PROFESSOR. What's the matter. Begum, you'd think you'd swallowed a tenpenny nail. [*To* PEGGY.] A glass of water, pigeon.

MRS. SCALLY *grabs hold of him, runs him backwards, and shoots him into the room. He is heard falling.*

MRS. SCALLY. There's a glass of water for you! [*She picks up hat, coat, and suitcase, pitches them into the room.*] Now! we'll see who's mistress here. . . .

PEGGY. Somebody coming in.

MRS. SCALLY *smooths hair and dress and goes to back door.* MRS. KILROY *comes in. She is a big, vain countrywoman, aged forty-five, and dressed in her very best.*

MRS. SCALLY. W-ell, Mrs. Kilroy! At last! [*They kiss lightly.*] It's a shame to bring you in this way, but the parlour's turned upside-down for the Professor coming. . . .

MRS. KILROY. This is perfection. Nothing would do Mr. Kilroy but I should come over and see Peggy. He has raved all afternoon about Peggy. And as for Joseph, I declare the boy's half crazy.

MRS. SCALLY. This is Peggy herself . . . just in

her apron. Peggy darling, this is Mrs. Kilroy.

MRS. KILROY [*kissing* PEGGY]. Your girls are all very good-looking, Mrs. Scally, but Peggy's the pick of the bunch.

MRS. SCALLY. The people say that, anyway. The others take more after the Scallys, but Peggy favours my own people. She has the Professor's eyes.

MRS. KILROY. Well, Peggy, dear, I hope you'll make Joseph a good wife. He's very young and wild and foolish, but you're a good sensible girl.

PEGGY. I'll do my best.

MRS. KILROY. That pleases me better than big promises. After all, it's a great lottery.

MRS. SCALLY. Put off your things, Mrs. Kilroy.

MRS. KILROY. I'll put off this jacket, for I'm warm. But I'll keep on my hat. We haven't long to stay. [*She takes jacket off, showing a formidable dress and jewellery.*]

MRS. SCALLY [*takes jacket*]. I'll leave this in the hall. Peggy, get Mrs. Kilroy a comfortable chair. [*She goes out.*]

MRS. KILROY. Peggy dear, won't Rush Hill make a lovely home for you and Joseph?

PEGGY. Beautiful. [*Gets her a chair.*]

MRS. KILROY [*sits*]. I want to ask you one thing before your mother comes in. Joseph says Hugh O'Cahan walked in here this morning and threw down your presents and told you to make jam of them. Is that true?

PEGGY. Quite true, Mrs. Kilroy.

MRS. KILROY. Well, that relieves my mind more than I can say. . . . I hear he's going off to-night, so you're rid of him for life and for ever. Do you happen to know where he's going?

PEGGY. Australia, I think.

MRS. KILROY. That's the place for him. The farther away the better. For I'd be afraid of Joseph quarrelling with him. Joseph's that hasty — like his father.

MRS. SCALLY *comes in and locks room door after her.*

MRS. SCALLY [*sits*]. Are the men not coming in?

MRS. KILROY. Oh, they'll be looking at the cattle. Joseph's a great judge of cattle. He was at the College, you know. [*To* PEGGY] Peggy dear, would you mind telling them to come in?

PEGGY. With pleasure. [*She goes out.*]

MRS. KILROY. We haven't long to stay, for Mr. Kilroy has a meeting to-night.

MRS. SCALLY. Your husband's a very busy man.

MRS. KILROY. Fearful! I hardly ever see him. Fairs and markets and Council meetings. . . . You may guess, one of the children asked him the other day, " Daddy, where do you live? "

MRS. SCALLY. He's a great man.

MRS. KILROY. And he thinks you're a great business woman. Of course, I've heard many a one praising your management. So I want to ask you about the match. Are you satisfied?

MRS. SCALLY. I was so from the first. But what about yourself, are you content?

MRS. KILROY. Now that I've seen Peggy and talked to her, I'm more than content; I'm pleased and happy.

MRS. SCALLY. Thank goodness! We'll have the wedding immediately.

MRS. KILROY. That brings me to what I want to say, Mrs. Scally. James — I won't call him Mr.

Kilroy to you — tells me you've a brother a professor coming here.

MRS. SCALLY. Yes, I'd a letter this morning.

MRS. KILROY. Where does he usually reside?

MRS. SCALLY. He travels a great deal.

MRS. KILROY. James said he thought he was a professor in Edinburgh University.

MRS. SCALLY. No, I don't think he's stationed there. He travels a great deal in foreign countries.

MRS. KILROY. Well, dear, you'll maybe think me a very vain woman. But I'd like to've the Professor at the wedding. It would give a tone to it and lift it above the ordinary country wedding.

MRS. SCALLY. I'd like to have him there myself, but it mightn't fit in with his plans.

MRS. KILROY. Could we not make our plans to fit in with his?

MRS. SCALLY. Perhaps we could. I'll see. If it can possibly be arranged I'll have him at the wedding.

MRS. KILROY. That's grand. I'm glad I mentioned it. Now I'm content.

PEGGY *comes in.*

PEGGY. They're coming in. They were looking at the new binder.

MRS. KILROY. Yes, Joseph's a great one for machinery.

KILROY, JOSEPH, *and* JOHN *come in.* JOHN *has on his black coat and hat.*

KILROY. Well, have you ladies had a good crack about the latest hats and all the falderals?

MRS. KILROY. We never mentioned a hat, James,

nor a falderal. But we'd a very pleasant talk, just the same.

KILROY [*slapping his wife's shoulder*]. Doesn't this caretaker of mine wear well?

MRS. SCALLY. Remarkable! She's still the best-looking woman and the best put-on woman comes into the chapel.

KILROY. Do you hear that, Ellen? [*Slaps.*] And that's from a lady that flatters nobody. [*Slaps.*] She's as good as new, Bridget.

MRS. KILROY. Sit down now and behave yourself. If I was gone you'd have a young one before a week.

KILROY. Haha! She wouldn't say that so gaily if she believed it.

MRS. SCALLY. Not a bit of her. . . . Now, Peggy, make the tea.

PEGGY *sees them all seated at the table, then starts making tea.*

JOHN. Make it strong, Peggy. I want a good strong cup. [*Holds his head.*]

MRS. SCALLY. Joseph, you're very quiet.

MRS. KILROY. That's because I'm here.

JOSEPH [*mutters*]. Awwwwwh! [*Hangs his head.*]

MRS. SCALLY [*takes a bottle of wine and glasses from cupboard*]. This won't make anybody drunk, it's only wine. Peggy, will you've some?

PEGGY. No, thanks, mother: I'll wait and have tea.

MRS. SCALLY. All right, dear. [*Puts round the wine.*]

KILROY [*stands up*]. I'm not going to make a speech. I'm only going to say a few words. Bridget, I want you and my Ellen to be great friends. Very great friends. In fact, this wedding'll make us more than friends, it'll make us near relations.

MRS. SCALLY. Hear, hear!

KILROY. With your own two farms and Rush Hill all lying in together, we practically own the landscape. . . .

PROFESSOR *makes a racket at the room door.*

PROFESSOR [*off*]. Open this door!

KILROY [*shudders and tries to proceed*]. We'll drink now to the prosperity of the young couple. That they may . . . may . . . may——

PROFESSOR [*gives door a heavy thud*]. Open up, you clodhoppers! Or I'll batter it down.

MRS. SCALLY [*in desperation*]. Go on, James! Go on with your speech.

KILROY. That they may . . . may . . . always . . . always have the grace . . . always——

PROFESSOR [*delivers another crash*]. Open! Open this door!

MRS. KILROY [*frightened*]. In God's name, who's that!

PROFESSOR [*off, loudly*]. It's me! Professor Tim! Sister Bridget has me locked in — trying to hide me. [*Kicks the door.*]

KILROY. Ah, Mrs. Scally! [*Collapses on chair.*]

MRS. SCALLY [*rising*]. I may as well tell you the truth, Mrs. Kilroy. It's my brother, and he's no credit to me. He's not the man I expected.

MRS. KILROY. Not the Professor, is it?

PROFESSOR [*off*]. It is the Professor! Open up and I'll show you who it is. [*Kicks door.*]

JOHN. You may as well open the door, Bridget.

MRS. SCALLY. He's not presentable.

JOHN. If you don't open the door he'll present himself.   He'll come through it.

MRS. SCALLY [*goes to door*]. Lie down on the sofa, Tim, and rest yourself.   We've visitors.

PROFESSOR. Open up!   Amn't I a visitor too?

MRS. SCALLY. Ah, this is cruel.   [*She opens the door and the* PROFESSOR *comes in.*]

PROFESSOR. You thought you'd killed me, Bridget. Eh?

MRS. SCALLY. Whisht, now . . . you tripped over something.

PROFESSOR. I tripped over nothing at all.   You gimme a heave that sent me heels over tip.   Here, feel this lump.   [*On his head.*]

MRS. SCALLY. Nonsense, Tim.   You only imagine things.

PROFESSOR. Imagination doesn't raise a lump on a man's head like an onion.   [*Fingers lump gingerly.*]

MRS. SCALLY. Your head's all wrong.

PROFESSOR. My head was all right till you smashed it.   [*Draws knife.*]   For two pins I'd slit you.

MRS. KILROY [*screams*]. Oh, James! he's a knife.

MRS. SCALLY *backs away and* PEGGY *goes to* PROFESSOR.

PEGGY. Give me that knife, uncle.   [*Gets it.*]   I'll keep it for you.

PROFESSOR. Keep it safe, pigeon;   for that's the knife I cut my food and baccy with.

PEGGY. Come and sit down.

PROFESSOR [*comes to table*]. Hullo, all!   Who's the smashing big heifer in the hat?

MRS. KILROY [*afraid*]. James!

KILROY. It's all right, Ellen.   He'll not touch

you. [*To* PROFESSOR] That's my wife, sir. Isn't she a good specimen?

PROFESSOR. Of what?

KILROY. Of an Irishwoman.

PROFESSOR. Begum, she's like a Burmese idol.

MRS. KILROY [*jumps up*]. James Kilroy, I'm going out of this place!

PROFESSOR. Sit down, dear; sit down. I won't eat you. You're not my style of muslin.

MRS. KILROY. How dare you speak to me!

KILROY. Now, Ellen——

MRS. KILROY. James Kilroy, you and your son told me a parcel of lies! You told me this man was a professor in Edinburgh University——

PROFESSOR. Begum, he didn't stint you in that one.

MRS. KILROY. And Mrs. Scally backed you up in deceiving me. [*To* MRS. SCALLY] You and your professor! A drunken sailor! [*Marches out, back.*]

KILROY [*rising*]. Come back, Ellen. Don't go away. [*To* MRS. SCALLY] Bridget, get this man out of sight. Put him in the churn and put the lid on him. . . . I'll fetch Ellen back in a minute. [*He goes out.*]

PROFESSOR. I'm tired. [*Sits.*]

JOSEPH. Peggy, will this matter to you and me?

PEGGY. Not to me, Joseph.

JOSEPH. No, nor to me. I don't care if the Professor was ten times as bad a case. Nor my father doesn't care——

PROFESSOR. Nor your mother won't care either, Joseph, when she hears what your father has to say. . . . She'll come in and eat out of my hand.

MRS. SCALLY. Tim, I'll forgive you a lot if you go and lie down in the room for half an hour.

PROFESSOR. I don't think you've very much to forgive.   I think I'm the injured party.

KILROY *and* MRS. KILROY *come in.   He is red and embarrassed, she a little crestfallen.*

KILROY. We're all right now.   Sit down, Ellen. [*He and* MRS. KILROY *resume their places at table.*]

PROFESSOR. Mrs. . . . Mrs. Kilroy, I apologise. I'll behave myself like a gentleman and a scholar.

KILROY. There now, Ellen.   He won't bother us again.   [*Takes up his glass.*]   Come on now.   Let's all be the best of friends.   Here's luck and prosperity and wedding bells.   Drink up, Ellen.   [*All drink.*]

PEGGY. Uncle, will you have some wine?

PROFESSOR. No, dear, I've the pledge for life.

MRS. SCALLY. Tea, Peggy.

PEGGY *is pouring out tea when* ALLISON *comes in.*

ALLISON. Well, Professor, are you still here?

PROFESSOR. No, I'm at sea.

KILROY. Nothing wrong, Mr. Allison?

ALLISON. Not a thing the matter, James.   The bank only wants this agreement signed by you and John Scally to-night.

JOHN. Me! what does the bank want me to sign?

MRS. SCALLY. Silence, John!

JOHN. This is too serious for silence!   [*To* ALLISON] What business have you or the bank with me?

MRS. SCALLY. James Kilroy bought Rush Hill on the understanding that you'd go in with him as bailsman.

JOHN. James Kilroy never mentioned the like to me.

MRS. SCALLY. He mentioned it to me! I said you'd do it and you shall!

JOHN. Well, I'm cursed if I shall!

PROFESSOR. Bully Johnny!

JOHN. I'll sign no bills! No bills. [*Sits.*]

MRS. SCALLY. Mr. Allison, have you the paper here?

ALLISON. Yes, ma'am. [*He takes a paper from attaché case.*]

MRS. SCALLY. Hand it to me and a pen.

ALLISON [*gives her both*]. Your husband signs *there.*

PROFESSOR. Now, Johnny: you're going to get your new spine tested.

MRS. SCALLY [*places pen and paper under* JOHN's *nose*]. John Scally, you've never disobeyed me since the morning I married you. I told James Kilroy to buy Rush Hill and you would sign this paper. He's making a good home for your daughter. Now then. Take the pen in your hand and write your name. . . .

JOHN [*wavering*]. I'd rather not, Bridget——

MRS. SCALLY. Lift the pen!

JOHN [*with trembling hand obeys*]. I know nothing about banks or bills——

MRS. SCALLY. Write your name!

JOHN [*hesitating*]. I know in my heart I shouldn't do this. . . .

PROFESSOR. Johnny Scally: if you sign that paper every small boy in the parish'll laugh at you.

JOHN [*throws down the pen and jumps up*]. I'm cursed over again if I sign it! [*Sweeps pen and paper and glasses off the table.*] Take the whole thing away to blazes and sign it yourselves!

PROFESSOR. Bully Johnny! that's the first time I've ever seen you in pants.

JOHN [*raging*]. I'll not be made a scarecrow of any longer! Nobody ever signed a bill for me and I'll sign nothing for no man! [*Sits down.*]

MRS. SCALLY. I'll not affront myself before these people, but I'll make you rue this night's work.

JOHN. From now on — from this very minute — you'll take your own place and I'll take mine! I'm no jinny!

PROFESSOR. Sit down, sister. Your despotic reign is over. Johnny's cock of the walk.

O'CAHAN *comes in, back. He is wearing a tweed suit and has an overcoat and suitcase.*

O'CAHAN. I'm sorry to interrupt the picnic. But I want a word with you, Mr. Allison.

ALLISON. Shall we go outside?

O'CAHAN. No, it isn't necessary. I'm going away now, and there's the keys of Rush Hill. That'll save you any trouble. [*Gives him a bunch of keys.*]

ALLISON. O'Cahan, you're a prince.

O'CAHAN. In reduced circumstances.

PEGGY *goes off quietly to the room.*

ALLISON. I've a car, Hugh. Won't you let me drive you to the town?

O'CAHAN. I'll be very glad of a lift. I don't think I ever walked to the town in my life. [*To* JOHN] John, I owe you forty pounds for a colt.

JOHN [*angrily*]. You owe me nothing! You buried the foal.

O'CAHAN [*takes out money*]. You couldn't help that. It might as readily have won the Derby.

There's your money. [*Lays it on table.*]

JOHN. Will you take a luckpenny?

O'CAHAN. A luckpenny for a dead foal? [*Smiling.*] Poor John! You're a decent one.

JOHN. Will you let me shake your hand itself?

O'CAHAN [*holding out his hand*]. I'm very glad you want to, John. [*They shake.*]

JOHN. Good-bye, Hugh. And remember this: John Scally knowd you from a child and liked you and respected you.

O'CAHAN. Thanks, John. You were a good neighbour.

PEGGY *comes in dressed for travelling.*

PEGGY. Now, Hugh, are you ready?

MRS. SCALLY [*jumps up*]. What! Where are you going?

PEGGY. I really don't know, mother: wherever Hugh's going.

PROFESSOR. Bully Peggy!

MRS. SCALLY. Peggy Scally, you're mad! You won't cross the threshold to-night.

PEGGY. Hugh, I'm going with you. Take me out of this.

O'CAHAN. I don't think anyone, Peggy, is going to stop you.

PROFESSOR. Now, Joseph, this is your last chance to get knocked out flat.

JOSEPH. Awwwwh!

MRS. SCALLY. John Scally, save your daughter. She won't heed me any more.

JOHN [*rising*]. Do nothing rash, Peggy. You're a good girl.

PEGGY. I'm doing nothing rash, father. I was

engaged to Hugh O'Cahan when he'd plenty. Now I'm going with him when he's nothing.

PROFESSOR. Begum, she's a thick-and-thinner.

JOHN. She put that plain and dacent. I'm proud of Peggy. . . . Hugh O'Cahan, you don't know what you're getting. It's not because she's my daughter I say this: no man in the world is good enough for Peggy Scally to clean her feet on.

O'CAHAN. I didn't think you knew that, John.

JOHN. But she's going with you, and I won't stop her. . . . [Blinking.] But, Lord, I wish you were staying at home, that I could see Peggy whiles. But here's a fair offer: stay here another week and get married proper, and I'll give Peggy her fortune.

O'CAHAN. Peggy's all the fortune I want, John. I'm going to throw off my coat and vest and work. [To the KILROYS] You people have got my old homestead. But if I live I'll come back and root you out of it. If I die, a son of mine'll come back and root you out of it. But I believe I'll come back and do it myself. I just feel that way about it.

PROFESSOR. That's inspiration. If a man hold on to that he can crush the earth like an egg-shell. He can break the wheel that tried to break him.

JOHN. Peggy, you and me were always the best of friends. I never seen your frown. Will you make Hugh wait here another week?

PEGGY. Hugh, we'll do as father says.

O'CAHAN. Right, Peggy. You're the law and the prophets.

JOHN. Hugh O'Cahan, I'll say out before all these people what was always in my mind. I always had a great grah for you. It did me good to meet you on the road. You were a wild fella but a good fella. You as good as gimme a brown mare that made me a power of money with her foals. . . .

o'cahan. Never mind about the brown mare. Tell us some of the wild deeds.

john. You went too fast, Hugh. That's the short way of putting it.

professor. That takes in wine, women, and cards——

john. And leppin' horses.

o'cahan. How much do you reckon I've spent on all those wild things since Uncle Hugh died?

john. Some says fifty thousand, and some twice that.

o'cahan. Mr. Allison, how much has the bank got against Rush Hill?

allison. Four thousand pounds.

o'cahan. How much had the bank against it when Uncle Hugh died?

allison. The same — four thousand pounds.

o'cahan. There you are, John. It isn't hard to earn a local reputation for riotous living. As a matter of fact I never — well, let the dead O'Cahans lie.

professor. Come and sit down, Hugh. Begum, I'm proud of my race.

o'cahan. So am I. [*Sits.*]

kilroy [*rising*]. Mr. Allison, I want to speak to you. Come outbye. [*He and* allison *go out.*]

peggy [*takes off coat and hat*]. Shall I pour out the tea, mother?

professor. Begum, she's a cool one. . . .

mrs. kilroy. No tea for me. My jacket, please!

MRS. SCALLY. I'll get it. [*She goes out.*]

MRS. KILROY. Go, Joseph, and put the horse in the trap. You've had a very narrow escape.

JOSEPH [*going*]. I've Rush Hill anyway. And I can marry any girl I like in three counties. I don't want nobody's leavings. [*At the door.*] Look at this circus!

As JOSEPH *goes out* MOLL *and* PADDY *come in.* MOLL *is sniffing audibly. She has on the new hat and dress, carries an ungainly bundle, and has a cat in a basket.* PADDY *is festooned with a saddle and bridle and other riding tackle.*

MOLL. We've seen the last av him, and the last av Rush Hill. [*Sniffs.*] We're all homeless this night, and broken-hearted as a motherless colt. May the holy saints — Colum, Patrick, and Bridget —be with him wherever he goes. . . .

O'CAHAN. The saints are all here, Moll.

MOLL. Oh, sweet heavens! gimme another look at you. [*Peering at him*] I can hardly see you for my crying eyes.

PEGGY [*placing a chair*]. Sit down, Moll, and take a good look at him. What have you got in the basket?

MOLL. Ach, sure it's the cat. Toby. We couldn't leave him behind us to be starved and beaten to death by the Kilroys. [*Sits.*] Och, hum!

PEGGY [*gets a chair*]. Sit down, Paddy. We're having tea.

PADDY [*sits*]. It's good to be all here — if only for a minute — as the swallows light on the road.

MRS. KILROY [*loudly*]. My jacket! My jacket!

MRS. SCALLY *comes in with it.*

MRS. SCALLY. This is getting a very distinguished gathering!

PROFESSOR. " Go ye out into the highways and byways," etc. etc.

JOHN. Bridget, don't be harsh. Moll Flanagan has the homeless cat in a basket. That's a lesson for us all.

MRS. SCALLY. John Scally, one would think I was a hard-hearted woman. Have I ever refused to give alms to a poor person at the door?

JOHN. Never, Bridget. Never.

MRS. SCALLY. If Peggy's going away I'll keep Moll Flanagan and the cat till they get a new home.

JOHN. And Paddy could give the boys a hand with the harvest.

PROFESSOR. And the cat could live on his wits.

PEGGY. Moll, I'm going away with Hugh. Will you stay here till I send for you?

MOLL. I will — if it was fifty years.

O'CAHAN. Paddy, you can hang about and give the Scally boys a hand with the horses. You'll hear from me in a very short time — if I'm living.

PADDY. Long or short, I'll be ready, boss. [*He pulls the hat down over his eyes.*]

PROFESSOR [*rising*]. Lucky devil, O'Cahan! Youth, love, friendship, and devotion, and the cat for luck. . . . My valise! where is my valise?

MRS. SCALLY. It's in the room.

PROFESSOR. Begum, I'm dry. [*He goes to the room.*]

MRS. KILROY. I'll take my jacket, Mrs. Scally. You'll soon have a fine collection of friends here. . . .

MRS. SCALLY [*giving her jacket*]. Thank God, there's plenty for them to eat. And if we want more we won't ask you to bail us.

JOHN. Holy tattler! That's a posey. Honour where honour's due. Outrageous, Bridget. Atrocious!

KILROY *and* ALLISON *come in*.

KILROY [*with a paper in his hand*]. Now, John Scally, as man to man, will you sign this paper?

MRS. SCALLY. He will not. John has more common sense than all in the house. I see now, what I didn't see before — that bail is a near-cut to the workhouse.

JOHN. Well put, Bridget. Well put.

KILROY. That ends it. [*Tears the paper.*] The deal's off, Allison. You can give Rush Hill to some of your own cronies. You never wanted me to get it.

ALLISON. I never wanted anybody to get it. I wanted it to remain with O'Cahan. And it does.

O'CAHAN. Mr. Allison, if you think that's a suitable jest——

ALLISON. It's no jest. I don't make cruel jests to an old friend in your position. [*He takes a thick bundle of ancient documents from attaché case.*] It's all here . . . deeds, documents, old mortgages, everything. [*Looks round.*] Where's the Professor?

PEGGY. He went to the room.

ALLISON. We people have been making sad fools of ourselves. Mrs. Scally, you should have known better——

MRS. SCALLY. Known what?

ALLISON. That your brother has all his life been an eccentric person. . . .

MRS. SCALLY. My God! has he been play-acting?

ALLISON. Yes, and doing it not badly. In him the stage has lost a great actor. He's a professor of Geology, and a considerable man in the world.

KILROY. The thing is — has he money?

ALLISON. On that point he was able to satisfy the bank, or I wouldn't have these papers.

KILROY. Where has he been for years?

ALLISON. I didn't ask him. Wherever he was he's just got back.

JOSEPH *comes in, his eyes popping.*

JOSEPH. The Lord save us! There's a waggon-load of stuff come for the Professor — trunks, bags, golf sticks, and fishin' rods — like a load of hay! [*He flings out again.*]

MRS. SCALLY. Is the stuff coming here?

ALLISON. I don't know a thing about it. I only saw it piled up on the platform.

PROFESSOR *comes in wearing a baggy tweed suit and a crumpled tweed hat with many trout flies in it.*

PROFESSOR. I've some luggage at the front door, but I told the man to wait. Part of it is going over to Rush Hill, and part of it staying here. [*With a dry smile.*] I've been enjoying myself.

ALLISON. At our expense.

PROFESSOR. A dozen years up-country makes a man thirsty for a joke. Tribesmen have no sense of humour. Their one bit of pastime is throat-cutting.

ALLISON [*hands over papers*]. You've got everything there, deeds and mortgages. Some of them haven't seen daylight for a hundred years.

JOSEPH *comes in and stands by with his mouth open.*

G

PROFESSOR. Give me the keys. [*Gets keys from* ALLISON.] Come here, Peggy. . . . To-day you gave me a kindly greeting and three pound notes. Do you remember?

PEGGY. Y-yes.

PROFESSOR. At the time it looked a bad investment, but you cast your bread on the waters. [*Gives her the keys and papers.*] That's a wedding present.

PEGGY [*her lip trembling*]. I'm going to cry. . . .

PROFESSOR. Not just now, if you please. You've all night to cry.

PEGGY. Can I do with these things whatever I like, uncle?

PROFESSOR. That you can, Peggy. Keep them, give them away, or light your pipe with them.

PEGGY. Can I give them to Hugh?

PROFESSOR. I know of nothing to hinder you.

PEGGY [*hands them to* O'CAHAN]. You said you'd come back home, Hugh, didn't you? [*No reply.*] You were a good prophet: without going away you're coming back. . . . Now, say something.

O'CAHAN *damps his lips and shakes his head. He has no words.*

PROFESSOR. Young man, your silence is more eloquent than a speech by Pericles.

PEGGY. Try again, Hugh. [*He shakes his head. To* PROFESSOR] Of late he hadn't many windfalls.

PROFESSOR. That's obvious. Like the bear, he behaves better in defeat.

O'CAHAN [*shrugs*]. I could speak, if I knew what to say. I'm as bewildered as a man in a dream. [*Pause.*] Now everything I want to say must remain unexpressed. . . . The last ten days, one crash coming after another. . . . Leaving Rush Hill to-night was like walking out to be hanged.

PROFESSOR. Every young man at least once should stand on the brink of ruin, with no living soul to care whether he goes over the edge. That experience is an education——

O'CAHAN. And a costly one.

PROFESSOR. Everything worth while is costly. [*Pause.*] If you and Peggy should have sons, which is not unlikely, call one Timothy. That's my fee.

PADDY. In sowl, we'll call half a dozen Tim.

MOLL. Paddy! have some morals.

PROFESSOR. Still a few salmon trout in the river, Hugh?

O'CAHAN. It's stiff with them.

PROFESSOR. I'll thin them out. For the rest of my life I want to go fishing every day. I'll spend half time at Rush Hill and the other half here with the Scallys. Can I have a room facing the south?

O'CAHAN. Can Peggy and I've a room facing anywhere? The rest of the house belongs to you.

PROFESSOR. With Peggy the undisputed boss of the show. You hear that, Peggy?

PEGGY. I do, uncle. I hope Hugh hears it too. I want no more double-banks or stone walls. . . .

PADDY. That means no leppin'.

O'CAHAN. Before all present, Peggy, I hand you the whip and the reins.

PADDY. Gimme them keys, boss.

O'CAHAN [*hands them to him*]. Hurry home, Paddy, and turn up the lights. I'll be after you directly.

PADDY. Come on, Moll Flanagan; get into your gear. I'm sorry I bought you all that finery.

MOLL [*struggling to her feet*]. Ah, sweet God! the

torrents av joy are killing me. . . .

PROFESSOR. Paddy Kinney.

PADDY. Yes, your honour.

PROFESSOR. To-day you gave me half a dollar.

PADDY. Ah, God forgimme! sure I thought you were as poor as myself.

PROFESSOR. I'll make you a suitable present if you kiss Moll Flanagan in that hat and frock.

PADDY [drops the saddle]. By my sowl, I'll earn that present. . . .

MOLL [protecting herself with the basket]. Daar ye!

PADDY. Your basket av cats won't save ye, me-lady! [He swarms in and kisses her.] Ye might as well try to kiss a menagerie.

PROFESSOR. Besides the present, Kinney, I'll furnish a cottage if you marry Moll Flanagan inside thirty days.

PADDY. Thirty days, is it? Within a week I'll lead her up the aisle!

MOLL. I'll not be hard to lead. I'll be three good steps in front av ye.

PADDY. Come on, then. You're going to get a good husband after all. . . . Turn your head for home, and break into a nice steady trot. [He drives MOLL out in front of him.]

KILROY. Ellen, we may as well go too.

PROFESSOR. James Kilroy, you're a good Irishman. You put a pound note in my hand at the station. Sit down and smoke a cigar.

JOHN. Sit down, James, and forget all about it. As Tim says, you're a good Irishman.

KILROY. Thank you. [Sits.]

PROFESSOR. Peggy, you'll find a box of cigars in my valise.

PEGGY. Right, uncle. [*Goes to the room.*]

PROFESSOR. Hugh, would you mind telling Peggy it's a flat box I want?

O'CAHAN [*going*]. The flat box . . . the flat box. [*He goes out.*]

ALLISON. May I stay and have a smoke?

PROFESSOR. I was just about to invite you.

ALLISON. Thanks. [*Sits down.*]

MRS. KILROY. Joseph, keep up your heart. Mrs. Scally has more daughters than Peggy.

JOSEPH. I'd marry any one of the other three. I know the fat one. . . .

PROFESSOR. Joseph, you're what's called a marrying man.

JOSEPH. Yes, sir. I'm twenty-one.

PROFESSOR. Well, take my advice and do it now, or the urge may not come again for many years. Then — unless a widow with a numerous family — no female would look at you.

PEGGY *comes in with cigars, followed by* O'CAHAN, *who hands her a side-comb.*

PEGGY. Joseph, you ought to set your hat for Susan.

JOSEPH. Is that the short, fat one?

PEGGY. Yes, she isn't very tall. She likes you.

JOSEPH. And I'm mad about her! Will you put in a word for me, Peggy?

PEGGY. I will, Joseph.

JOSEPH. Mrs. Scally, will you speak to Susan for me?

MRS. SCALLY. I'll see, Joseph. [*Subdued.*] If God spares me, I mean to talk less. [*Going*] I'll go now and lie down half an hour, I'm feeling upset. . . .

PEGGY [*flings her arms round her neck*]. Mother, don't leave us! [*Sets her down and kisses her.*] Sure you've made us all what we are. . . . Hugh, come and kiss mother.

PROFESSOR. That's an ordeal. The champion stone wall.

O'CAHAN. I'll face it. [*He kisses her.*] You're the only living thing I was ever afraid of. Do you know why? Because I often had reason to be ashamed of myself.

MRS. SCALLY. God bless you, Hugh. I was always anxious about Peggy.

JOHN. By the hedges, it's grand! It's outrageous! Atrocious! It's a fittin' epitaph.

PEGGY. And Uncle Tim's had his joke, mother. In the rôle of a drunken sailor he must have known what to expect.

PROFESSOR. I got off in a coach. . . . Shake hands, sister Biddy. [*They shake.*] Like every good Irish mother you've got a sharp tongue and a large vocabulary, and it takes both to bring up a big family of boys and girls.

MRS. SCALLY [*drying her eyes*]. We've seven of the best children in the world.

JOHN. As straight as seven dies.

PROFESSOR. Glad to hear it. And glad to be home. As Johnny says, it's a fitting epitaph. [*Opens the box.*] Have a smoke, friends. I bought these cigars in Bombay.

THE END

PAUL TWYNING

A Comedy in Three Acts

Paul Twyning was first produced at the Abbey Theatre, Dublin, on October 3, 1922, with the following cast:

PAUL TWYNING, *a Tramp Plasterer* . .	Barry FitzGerald
JAMES DEEGAN, *a Farmer and Magistrate* .	Gabriel J. Fallon
DAN DEEGAN, *his Son*	M. J. Dolan
PATRICK DEEGAN, *another Son, a Publican* .	P. J. Carolan
MRS. DEEGAN, *his Wife*	May Craig
JIM DEEGAN, *their Son*	Tony Quinn
DENIS M'GOTHIGAN, *a Farmer* . . .	Eric Gorman
ROSE M'GOTHIGAN, *his Daughter* . .	Eileen Crowe
DAISY MULLAN, *a returned American* . .	Christine Hayden
MR. O'HAGAN, *a Solicitor*	Peter Nolan

ACTS I and III.—James Deegan's kitchen.
ACT II.—Pat Deegan's public-house.

The play was produced by Lennox Robinson.

ACT I

JAMES DEEGAN'S *new kitchen. The walls are raw and the doors and windows unfinished.*

At the back are a door and two windows to the farm-yard; another door, left, to rooms. The fireplace is on the right, and a little beyond it is a cupboard built in the wall.

A table, an armchair, and a few ordinary chairs have been brought over from the old house and are piled up in a corner.

It is a July night, about dusk. PAUL TWYNING, *in white jacket and overalls, is mixing mortar on the floor with a shovel.* Old DEEGAN, *a tall, grave old man, dressed in Gladstonian style, comes in from the yard.*

DEEGAN. Paul Twyning, I want to speak a word.

PAUL. Yes, your worship.

DEEGAN [*irritably*]. I've told you repeatedly not to " worship " me, sir. I'm not on the Bench now.

PAUL. Well, sure I can't bring myself to address you like an ordinary man. Let me call you " your honour " itself. Sure, south of the Boyne, a big man like yourself — a farmer and magistrate — is called " your honour ", and looks for it.

DEEGAN. We in the North are more democratic.

PAUL. I hadn't noticed it.

DEEGAN. When will you be through with the plastering?

PAUL. In three or four days, master, if I'm spared the health. I'm now at the cornish in the parlour-

99

room, and, as you see, I'm working overtime and attending myself.

DEEGAN. The sooner you're finished and out of this, the better.

PAUL. Of coorse. That's a tradesman's thanks the world over.

DEEGAN. When I took you in — a tramp off the highway — it was to plaster my house, not to meddle in my family affairs.

PAUL. Is your honour joking?

DEEGAN. No, sir, I'm serious.

PAUL. And when and how did I meddle in your family affairs?

DEEGAN. You'd my son Daniel at a dance in M'Gothigan's barn and without my permission.

PAUL. But your other son Pat, that has the pub in the town, was at the dance himself and supplied the drink.

DEEGAN. That was a business transaction. Besides, Patrick is a married man, but this lad at home is single.

PAUL. But the M'Gothigans are respectable people, and your lad, as you call him, is over forty years of age.

DEEGAN. My son Daniel is — like all the young men of his generation — graceless and without understanding.

PAUL. Well, of coorse, I only know him a short time, your honour, but I'd formed a very high opinion of Dan.

DEEGAN. No doubt. But a tramp's opinion of respectability and mine are different. [*Sternly*] I don't want a daughter-in-law of your choosing, sir!

PAUL. Nor, I suppose, of Dan's either?

DEEGAN. You have said it. Daniel will have no choice. I'm going now to interview a suitable female to be his wife, and if she suits me she'll have to suit him, and you, and the M'Gothigans. [*He goes out.*]

PAUL. Well, begorry, I've tramped England, Ireland, and parts of Scotland, but there is the worst specimen of the landed aristocracy I've met. That's the sort of democrats the Land League left behind it. [*Shouts*] Hi, Dan! You may emerge from your rat-hole. Ould Clanricarde has gone out.

DAN *comes in; a wild-looking person, with hair turning from grey to whiteness. He is clothed a few degrees worse than a hired servant, and moves with quick, furtive gestures.*

DAN. What did my fader say, Paul? In God's name, amen.

PAUL. Well, he seems to think, Dan, you've been sporting your figure at M'Gothigan's dance.

DAN. Flames, has he heard I was there? What did he say? Did he mention Rose? Quick man, for your sowl, and tell a buddy.

PAUL. Oh, he knows all about your love-affair, Dan. But, I must say he took a very broad view of it. He says what is very true — that you have to marry sometime, and why not now?

DAN. My sowl, that is a broad view.

PAUL. He also says that you were always a headstrong lad, and he supposes if you've made Rose M'Gothigan a promise that you'll stick to it.

DAN [*excited*]. Did he say that, Paul? Did he call me a stubborn fella?

PAUL. Stiff-necked and stubborn were the words he used.

DAN. I'm in flames, but he's right! I was always as stiff as a mule if I took a thing in my head. But I didn't speak the word to Rose.

PAUL. Eh? Is that the next of it? Let you answer me a few questions. Didn't you sit beside her last night till the cocks were crowing this morning?

DAN. I did, heth.

PAUL. And didn't you hold her hand for hours at a stretch?

DAN. I'll never deny it.

PAUL. And didn't you slip her a conversation lozenger with the inscription upon it:

> " I love you very dearly,
> And if you love me,
> In spite of wind and weather
> We shall married be."

DAN. I did, heth, and she read it and laft her fill.

PAUL. And then you've the nerve to stand there and tell me you're not engaged?

DAN [confused]. Does Rose think I axed her?

PAUL. She does surely. And, what's far more important, her father and mother both maintain that you asked her.

DAN. Flames! has it went that far?

PAUL. But they all know the sort of James Deegan, J.P. They know you can't bring a woman in here without his consent.

DAN. Would Rose and her fader and mother agree to wait?

PAUL. Rose is only in the bud, and can afford to wait as long as you like.

DAN. Then, I'm in flames, but that settles it! I'll see Rose this night and make the match complete. That's the sort of me. If I made up my mind to do a thing, I always tore through it like a mad bull wi' the cholic.

PAUL. Now that's bould, headstrong talk. I like the way you lowered your brows when you said that. I never saw a more determined face in my life.

DAN [*lowering his brows*]. I can look very detarmint when I like. I wish I'd done it twenty-five years ago. I've been the wee boy too long.

PAUL. Well, Dan, I think that will do for the present. [*Looks about the floor.*] See if I left my spatula in the room. [DAN *goes out.*] Poor Dan! Your battering-ram expression will change quickly once ould Bismarck comes in.

DAN [*comes in with spatula*]. Is that your bottle in the room, Paul?

PAUL. That's a souvenir of M'Gothigan's dance. Fetch it here, Dan, and we'll celebrate your betrothal.

DAN *goes to the room and returns with a bottle.*

DAN [*spelling the name on the label*]. " Patrick Deegan . . . Boar's Head, Ballybullion." . . . This is my brother's whiskey, Paul.

PAUL. It's nothing the better of that, Dan. Get a cup. [DAN *gets a cup and* PAUL *pours him a dose.*] Toss it off quickly now, before it explodes in your face.

DAN. Here's to Rose herself, Paul. Angels guard her, amen. [*Drinks and twists violently.*] I'm in flames, but that's torpentine!

PAUL [*pours himself a drink*]. Here's every day to

you, Dan. May yourself and Rose live for ever.
[*Drinks.*] Sure enough, that's your brother's
whiskey. You might as well swallow a torchlight
procession.

DAN. He said he made it spacial for the dance.

PAUL. He put too much sheep-dip in it. Take it
away. [DAN *leaves bottle in room and comes back.*]
Get me some water for this cement.

DAN. Here's a bucket. [*Takes it and goes to the
yard.*] I'm away to the yard for water.

PAUL. Rose M'Gothigan ought soon to be showing up, if she hasn't renaged.

DAN [*rushes in*]. Paul Twyning! who's coming
down the road? All by her lone. Guess!

PAUL. Oh, I haven't the remotest idea. I give
it up.

DAN. Rose herself — may I never do what's sin-
ful! And taking every look at the new house. Now's
my chance, Paul.

PAUL. Tell me quickly: do you feel that nip of
whiskey in your head yet?

DAN. I feel it everywhere. It's flyin' up and
down to my feet. . . . Will I go out and put the
speak on her?

PAUL. And a nice posy y'are to put the speak on
anyone! Look at the dirt of your face. And where
is the blue dicky you wore at the dance?

DAN. It should be here. [*Takes an old rag of a
dicky from cupboard.*] I hid it in there this morning
when I come in from the dance.

PAUL. Well, put the dicky on your neck and give
the face a rub with a wet rag, and I'll invite Rose
in to see the house.

DAN. But what am I to say, Paul? How am I

to seal the match? I never did the like afore.

PAUL. I think I've a ring here that I picked up many years ago at Lisdoonvarna. [*Takes a ring from pocket.*] It mayn't be eighteen carat, Dan, but it's better than no ring at all. [*Gives it to him.*] Put that on her finger, and she's yours till the sands of the desert grow cold.

DAN. What finger, Paul? *will I put the finger Paul.*

PAUL. Oh, she'll hould out the correct finger, never fear.

DAN. But it doesn't fit, Paul?

PAUL. Then try some of the others. Put it on any finger it fits. The main thing is to get it on.

DAN. But what am I to say, Paul? How does other people do it?

PAUL. There's no cut-and-dry formula. Some do it with tears in their eyes, and others with their eyes tight shut. And some say one thing and some another. But in your case, something like this might do: " Rose, alanna, after long and serious consideration, I've decided to ask you to be Mrs. Dan Deegan. Now or never, Rose, will you marry me? "

DAN. Sowl, that's fine talk, Paul. You're a handy boy wi' the tongue.

PAUL [*going*]. When you're nicely groomed and the face scrubbed, sing a lilt of a song, and I'll fetch Rose in. [*He goes out.*]

DAN [*scrubbing his face*]. Rose, alanna, after long confederation, will you be Mrs. Dan Deegan? [*Shakes his head.*] That's not Paul's version of it. [*Struggling with dicky*] Confederation or conflageration. . . . Och, what odds about a word? She'll know what I mean. [*Gets dicky fastened and sings:*]

YOKE

" No pipe I'll smoke, no horse I'll ~~joke~~,
 Till my plough with rust turns brown:
 Till a smiling ~~maid~~, by my own fireside,
 Sits the Star of the County Down."

BRIDE

PAUL *and* ROSE *come in.   She is a rosy-cheeked girl,
aged twenty.*

PAUL. Dan, you've a voice like a piccolo.   About
a fortnight in Italy would make you perfect.

DAN. Och, you're only sconcin', Paul.   I wasn't
singing that well at all. [*Shaking hands with her.*]
Morra, Rose.   You're welcome there.   How are
you feeling after the ball?

ROSE. The best, Dan.   How's yourself?

DAN. Oh, as right as the mail. [*Shakes his head.*]
We'd a big night, Rose.   The biggest night ever
I put in.

ROSE. I'm glad you enjoyed yourself, Dan.
[*Looks round.*]   This is a fine big kitchen.

DAN. Sowl, it's big enough.   It's like a gaol-
yard.

ROSE. It wants for nothing, Dan.

DAN. Oh, it's very complete.

PAUL. Now that's where you're wrong, the pair
of you.   It's by no means complete; it wants the
main feature.   Wait and I'll explain what I mean.
[*Brings the old armchair to the fireside.*]   Now, my
decent girl, let you subside into that chair——

ROSE. Oh, Paul, I haven't a minute.

PAUL. But I won't keep you a second.   I only
want to let Dan see what I'm driving at. [ROSE *sits
down.*]   There now.   The kitchen is no longer a
gaol; 'tis a home, sweet home.

DAN [*chuckling*].   Sowl, Paul, it takes yourself.

PAUL. Now, Rose, I'll ask you one simple question. If Dan was alone in the world, wouldn't you be content to fill that chair for life and for ever?

ROSE. I suppose I would.

DAN. And it's my mother's chair too, Rose. Rest her in pace, amen.

PAUL. There you are now, Dan. Yourself and Rose are half engaged already. I'll give you a few minutes to put the seal on it, then I'll come back. [*He goes to the room, but is seen listening.*]

DAN [*after an awkward pause*]. This was a fine growing day, Rose.

ROSE. It looked like rain in the forenoon.

DAN. Ay, but it cleared up.

ROSE. We were working at the hay.

DAN. How's it cutting, Rose?

ROSE. Oh, fairly well, I think.

DAN. Ours is going to be light. [*Long pause.*] We'd a big night last night, Rose. You were the belle o' the ball.

ROSE. Oh, you're only saying that, Dan.

DAN. I'm sayin' the holy truth. You were the belle.

ROSE. The people were all remarking you and me talking, Dan.

DAN. Let them remark their fill. They'll maybe remark more than that afore long. [*After a painful effort.*] Rose, alanna, after long and serious confederation, will you be Mrs. Dan Deegan? Now or never, will you marry me?

ROSE. Oh, Dan, we needn't talk. . . .

DAN. For why, Rose?

ROSE. Because I haven't a penny, and with this grand house you'll be wanting a girl with a fortune.

DAN. Me want a fortune? Not the cross o' coin. You're a fortune yourself. You can feed pigs and milk cows and wash a dicky. That's enough for me.

ROSE. It's not enough for your father. He'll want money.

DAN. Well, my fader's over seventy. Can't we wait till he goes? All here is mine after his day. Pat has the wine-shop in the town.

ROSE. Well, Dan, I'll wait.

DAN. Och, I know'd you'd cave in at last. Love always finds a way. The ring's here and all. [*Puts it on her finger.*] You're Rose Deegan now, come weal or woe. It's a long time since I concaited ye.

PAUL [*comes in*]. Another match made in Heaven! My blessing, childer. [*Shakes hands.*] And now for a speedy marriage.

DAN. Oh, we've agreed to wait my fader's day, Paul.

PAUL. I heard the bargain, Dan. But that's only because you can't see your way sooner. With your father's consent and blessing you'd lose little time, I'll go bail.

DAN. Not a minute, Paul.

PAUL. Very well, then, just leave me to settle with your father. I think I can manipulate him. If I succeed I'll accept a small money present, say, five pounds — to carry me down to Carlow.

DAN. And you'll get it. A five-pound note. There's my hand. [*They shake.*]

ROSE [*making to rise*]. I'll be going now, Dan. Your father might come in.

DAN. Och, sit still, Rose. My fader won't be in this hour. He's away to look at the young heifers.

ROSE. I saw him going into Mullan's.

PAUL. It's maybe an *ould* heifer he'll look at before he comes back.

DAN [*alarmed*]. What d'ye mean, Paul Twyning?

PAUL. Isn't there an ould doll in the name of Mullan home from America with a boat-load of money?

DAN. I'm in flames but you're right! Ould Daisy Mullan.

PAUL. Well, Dan, herself is the heifer your father's gone to see. [*Listens.*] Whisht! And, begorry, she hasn't kept him long. He's in the yard. [*He runs off to the room.*]

DAN. My fader, my fader! as God's my judge, amen. . . .

ROSE [*leaps up*]. Oh, Dan, Dan!

DAN. Hide the ring, hide the ring!

DEEGAN *comes in.*

DEEGAN. Just so. I beg leave to be excused for coming in without knocking.

DAN [*shaking*]. I was only showing her the new house, fader.

DEEGAN. Did you tell her who built it?

DAN. Oh, the whole world knows that, fader. 'Twas yourself built it and paid it.

DEEGAN. How do you know whether it's paid or not?

DAN [*dashed*]. I hope it is, anyway.

DEEGAN. That's a good boy. Hope well and you'll have well. [*Glancing at chair*] You've been trying how Miss M'Gothigan would fit your mother's chair, I see.

DAN [*broken*]. She was only in it a minute, fader.

DEEGAN. And you've on your good dicky, I observe.

DAN. I only put it on after you went out, fader.

DEEGAN. Take it off, sir!

DAN. Yes, fader. [*Goes back and struggles with dicky.*]

DEEGAN. Does the new house suit you, Miss M'Gothigan?

ROSE [*choking*]. It's a fine house, sir.

DEEGAN. It will be a fine home for a young woman with certain qualifications. In those matters Daniel would be inclined to be rash, but I'll take care he makes no mistakes. Now I won't detain you. I bid you good evening.

ROSE. Good evening. [*Goes out sobbing.*]

DEEGAN [*wipes chair with his handkerchief and sits down*]. Come forward, boy.

DAN. Yes, fader. [*Stands in front of him.*]

DEEGAN. Is there anything between you and that low-born trull of Denis M'Gothigan's?

DAN. Not a ha'porth, fader. Thank God, amen.

DEEGAN. What authority had you to bring her into my house?

DAN. It was Paul Twyning, fader. He axed her in to see the plastering.

DEEGAN. And what authority had Paul Twyning to invite a strange female in here?

DAN. I don't know, fader. Him and the M'Gothigans is very pact. Maybe that was it.

DEEGAN. Paul Twyning and the M'Gothigans are much the same breed of inferiors. Tell Paul Twyning to come forth.

DAN. Yes, fader. [*Goes to room door and shouts.*] Paul Twyning, you're awanting. [PAUL *appears.*]

My fader wants you, Paul. [*Aside*] Not a word, Paul, for the love o' God, amen. I'm denying everything.

PAUL [*comes forward*]. Well, your honour, have you brought the ould aisy-chair across to the new hearth? Long may you fill it in comfort.

DEEGAN. Oh, thank you. It won't be long empty when I'm gone. Was it you invited that female M'Gothigan to inspect the house in my absence?

PAUL. I didn't see much harm in asking a decent girl to look at the plastering, God bless it. And, by the same token, I thought yourself was upstairs the while.

DEEGAN [*sharply*]. That will do, sir!

PAUL. What will do, sir?

DEEGAN. I want no more of that.

PAUL. Oh, very well, all right! [*Taking off jacket*] If you want no more of it, neither do I. Give me three days' pay and let me go back to my own country.

DEEGAN [*stands up*]. You've taken me up wrong, sir. I didn't mean you to stop work ; I meant you to stop lying.

PAUL. You're only making it worse. [*Flings jacket on floor.*] My three days' pay, or an apology! Suit yourself.

DEEGAN. An apology, for what?

PAUL [*loudly*]. For as good as calling me a liar! The devil recaive the spark of plaster I'll put on the wall till you apologise! And for a farden I'd plaster the house with writs for defamation of character.

DEEGAN. Writs! I've been in the Four Courts of Dublin in my time.

PAUL. And from what I hear you've dragooned

the whole parish ever since. But, by my sowl, you won't dragoon Paul Twyning! You were only a week-end in Dublin, but I was born and reared and educated in it.

DEEGAN. You're a credit to it. But go on with the plastering. I withdraw the offensive remark. Or perhaps you'd want a written apology?

PAUL. Oh, the verbal repudiation will satisfy my honour. But, since you've raised my dander, I'll press for my inalienable rights. As a journeyman I'm entitled to bring in any man, woman, or child to examine my work. That's how we tradesmen build up a reputation.

DEEGAN. Just so. Who will you invite next?

PAUL. Daisy Mullan's aunt, for one. She's a bedroom wants a new ceiling.

DEEGAN. Miss Mullan's aunt will be very welcome.

PAUL. And Denis M'Gothigan's pantry needs new lath and plaster. [*Picks up jacket.*] I'll have my full rights, or down tools. [*Goes to the room.*]

DEEGAN. That tramp scoundrel has more in his mind than plastering. . . . I hope you gave no promise of any kind to the slut?

DAN. No promise, fader. Thank God, amen.

DEEGAN. If you have, I'll deal drastically with you. I'll march you to Derry quay and put you aboard the emigrant ship with my own hands. Mind that.

DAN [*shivers*]. You wouldn't do that, fader dear.

DEEGAN. Try to thwart me, or disobey me, and you'll see. I've done it with your brothers and sisters when I was less independent than I am now. [*Holding up his hand*] Do you see that hand on my body?

DAN. Yes, fader.

DEEGAN. May it wither if I don't make an example of you!

DAN [*trembling*]. But I'm not trying to twart you, fader. I've no mind to twart you.

DEEGAN. Not to my face. But the moment my back is turned you've a dirty M'Gothigan cocked in your dead mother's chair. . . . May the Most High keep me in temper!

DAN. Amen, fader. Don't vex yourself, fader. I'll never marry nobody your day.

DEEGAN. You'll marry to-morrow if you're told! And the choice will be mine, not yours.

DAN. All right, fader. You're the best judge of a cow in the parish, and maybe of a well-doing woman too.

DEEGAN. If she has a certain amount of hard money I won't look too closely at her points. My thick-witted son is not such a catch in himself.

DAN. God knows that's true, fader.

DEEGAN. I have my eye on a suitable female for this chair. Like yourself, she's not embarrassed with too much intelligence; but I understand she has money.

DAN [*aghast*]. The ould Yankee Mullan! Ould Daisy Mullan, that could be my granny!

DEEGAN. You are wrong, sir. Miss Mullan is in the prime of life. [*Sternly.*] Would you dare to contradict me?

DAN [*meekly*]. Oh, whatever you plan yourself, fader, I'm agreeable. You're a highly educated man. And I know nothing, God help me. . . . But I don't like the Yankee twang.

DEEGAN. If her Yankee twang keeps you in the

far fields, so much the better. I'm not marrying you to be happy, or to sit with your feet in the ashes. . . . Go now and put on your Sunday clothes.

DAN. Where am I going, fader — in God's name, amen?

DEEGAN. You're going over with me to Mullan's. Wash the lime and mortar from behind your ears, and keep the cap pulled down over your hair. It's nice to see a boy of your age with grey hairs in his head!

DAN. I can't help my hair turning white, fader. . . . Will I put the dicky on my neck?

DEEGAN. Certainly so.

PAUL *comes in for mortar.*

PAUL. Dan, boys will be boys, and we all make mistakes. But I think you ought to take your distinguished father into your confidence. . . .

DAN. I'm in flames, but I'm betrayed! Sold like a bullock in Smithfield! [*Dashes off to the room.*]

PAUL. I may be only a tramp, your honour, but I've an Irish heart in my body; and it hurts me to see a foolish boy deceiving a good father.

DEEGAN. Paul Twyning, you are a better man than I gave you credit for. What has this lad been doing?

PAUL. He's been offering marriage to Rose M'Gothigan, and, needless to say, she accepted.

DEEGAN [*staggers*]. Oh, don't say that word! Tell me he has stolen something, or taken a false oath, but don't say he's pledged to that inferior.

PAUL. It grieves me to hurt a proud father's feelings, but I must protest the truth. He proposed to her in that aisy-chair a few minutes ago, and was accepted under my own eyes. . . .

DAN [*at room door*]. It's a lie, Judas! Mind, I'm prepared to fight for my life. It's your oath again mine, and what are you but a tramp from God knows where!

DEEGAN. Go inside, sir, and close the door! Leave my sight, lest Satan tempt me to lift my hand.

DAN. My oath's as good as Paul Twyning's.

PAUL. You could probably swear me out of court, Dan; but you can't swear your way through an engagement ring.

DAN [*loudly*]. Flames to the traitor! [*Goes in and bangs the door.*]

DEEGAN. Paul Twyning, be careful. A ring?

PAUL. A ring, your honour. He put it on her finger before I could run out and stop him.

DEEGAN. Would you swear to that?

PAUL. I couldn't do otherwise, your honour, and keep the conscience right.

DEEGAN [*drops into the easy-chair*]. Then Denis M'Gothigan has got a case against me at last.

PAUL. I'll leave you alone now with your grief, master. I'm glad I'd the moral courage to do my duty.

DEEGAN. Thank you.

PAUL [*knocks at room door*]. May I come in, Dan?

DAN [*off*]. Flames to the traitor!

PAUL *goes in.*

DEEGAN [*stands up*]. This has decided me. If Daisy Mullan has money . . .

DAISY *comes in; an oldish, over-dressed person with horn-rimmed glasses and much cheap jewellery. She has a large vanity-bag.*

DAISY. Mr. James Deegan, what do you think? I let you come away without getting your advice on several business propositions. First thing, I wanna ask about the Irish banking system. Are the Irish banks safe?

DEEGAN. Our leading banks are perfectly safe.

DAISY. And you think they'd give a gel a square deal if she was having her money crossed over from the States to this country, do you?

DEEGAN. Not the least doubt of it.

DAISY. Then I wanna know the best gamut for collecting my rents and having 'em remitted in case I buy me a shack and settle down here for a spell. Whatcha know about that, Mr. Deegan?

DEEGAN. That could easily be arranged.

DAISY. Say, you've taken a load off my shoulders. But ain't it just too bad my racing after you and blistering you with my troubles?

DEEGAN. No trouble, Miss Mullan, where you are concerned.

DAISY. I'll say you're a white man. [*Throws her eye over the place.*] So this is your new house, is it? And a mighty swell building it is. Large, airy, and commodious. Health to enjoy it, my friend.

DEEGAN. Thank you kindly. It's still in a raw state, or I would take you through it. The plasterer is still working in the room.

DAISY. Oh, that Dublin feller, eh? He's a good mechanic, ain't he? M'auntie's going to have him plaster a bedroom.

DEEGAN. Paul Twyning may have other faults, but he's a good tradesman.

DAISY. Hits the liquor, do he?

DEEGAN. He is by no means a sot. But he can't

keep his nose out of other people's business. He's been only three weeks in this locality, but he could write a history of the inhabitants. He questions the very children along the road as to their antecedents.

DAISY. Ain't that for you, now! And m'aunt she thinks him such an innocent babe. [*Opening bag*] Now for some more trouble, Mr. Deegan. I got an American bank draft here for a small amount, but seems I gotta have it endorsed by a responsible citizen before an Irish bank can fork out. Is that right?

DEEGAN [*chary*]. That I'm afraid is the rule. [*Puts on his specs.*]

DAISY [*fishes out a paper*]. This ain't it. This is my insurance policy on a block of house property I got on Mount Airy, West Philadelphia. [*Hands it to him.*] You hang on to that a moment, please, till I root out what I want.

DEEGAN. With pleasure. [*Scans document.*]

DAISY [*takes out another paper*]. What the heck have I got here? Why, yeah. My broker's receipts for a bunch of stock in the Chesapeake, Ohio, and Pennsylvania Railway. [*Hands it to him.*] I'll trouble you to hold it, Mr. Deegan.

DEEGAN. No trouble. [*Reads it.*]

PAUL *comes in and coughs to draw their attention.*

PAUL. Beg pardon. I'm sorry to interrupt the good work, but I want my spatula.

DEEGAN. No harm, Paul.

DAISY. Say, Mr. Twyning, when are you coming to plaster m'auntie's bedroom?

PAUL [*takes off his hat*]. About the fourth day from now, melady, if I'm spared the health.

DAISY. Well, that's a date. I'll tell m'auntie to've the room all cleared out.

PAUL. She may clear out the room, melady, but let her not order the material till I run my dimension-rule over the interior and give her an estimate.

DAISY. I'll sure tell her so. But, say, if you was in America and talk like that, you'd get fifteen dollars a day easy.

PAUL. I've a brother in Chicago — a lath and plasterer — making exactly that sum, melady. . . . But I mustn't retard the good work. [*Looks about floor.*] I thought my spatula was here. It must be outside. [*Goes out, back.*]

DAISY. Say, ain't he mannerable?

DEEGAN. He can pass himself very well.

DAISY [*takes out draft*]. Ah, here we are. It's only for three thousand dollars — about six hundred pounds. Have a look, Mr. Deegan, and see if it's correctly drawn.

DEEGAN [*examines it carefully*]. It's quite in order, Miss Mullan.

DAISY. Is there a bank in Ballybullion?

DEEGAN. Certainly so. And I do business there myself, and know the manager intimately.

DAISY. Why, dear Mr. Deegan, you're a prince.

DEEGAN [*returns papers*]. I'm going to town to-morrow morning, and I'll give myself the pleasure of driving you to the bank; and if you require my signature I'll be at your side.

DAISY. Why, my dear friend, I ain't got the education to thank you enough.

DEEGAN. No thanks at all, Miss Mullan. I'm very pleased to be able to serve you, and more than pleased to observe how well you have prospered abroad. [*Draws forward armchair.*] Take this chair, if you please, while I call my son Daniel.

DAISY [*sits down, laughing*]. Say, Mr. Deegan, you're so full of human kindness. You might put in a good word for me with your son Den or some other likely feller in the settlement. I always said I'd never marry a Yankee, and you bet I never will.

DEEGAN. I'm going to introduce you to my son Daniel. This house and ninety-five acres of freehold will be his portion. He's a good steady boy, free of all vice.

DAISY. Mr. Deegan, I hope you ain't joshing me. For I'm sure dead serious. Yes, sir: if you can offer me a live proposition like Den Deegan, I'm ready to prance right in and grab. I could put a few thousands into this ranch and make things hum like a bee-hive.

DEEGAN. Daisy Mullan, I'm not a frivolous man. I'm a serious man, and particularly serious in matters affecting my own house and family.

DAISY [*sets her hat*]. Then you can't have Den too speedy on the tape for mine. Is he in?

DEEGAN. He should be in the room. [*Pausing.*] I'll leave you together after the introduction. You may have to encourage him a little.

DAISY [*giggles*]. Gee! am I to do the sparking, am I?

DEEGAN. That will depend on how he behaves. [*Opens room door.*] Are you here, Daniel?

DAN [*off*]. Ay, I'm fixin' myself.

DEEGAN. You'll do very well. Come forth. [DAN *comes in in an ill-fitting ready-made suit.*] Miss Mullan, my son Daniel.

DAISY [*leaps up*]. Why, my! it's Den! Not a

shaving of differs since we was boy and gel at school. [*Grabs his hand*.]   And how is it, Den?

DAN [*smothering*]. Oh, fairish, fairish!

DAISY. And, like myself, Den, you ain't married yet.

DAN. Not yet — not yet.   Nor no notion of it. [*He backs away*.]

DAISY [*sits*]. Draw up a chair, Den, and let's have a gibber about the old school days.

DEEGAN [*after a pause*]. Come, boy: have you nothing to say for yourself?

DAN. I don't mind much about my school days. It's a long time ago.

DAISY. Well, sit right down, Den, and I'll stir up your recollection some.

DEEGAN [*placing another chair*]. Come forward, boy.

DAN [*aside*]. God help me now, amen. [*Sits down*.]

DEEGAN. Now, both of you are aware of what I have in mind.   So I want no delays.   Making a match is like swopping horses — the less one knows about the other, the better.   You have my permission to proceed.   [*He goes to the room*.]

DAISY. Say, Den, ain't this dinky?   A-setting at our own fireside, like Darby and Joan, ain't we? [*Draws chair closer*.]   What a swell picture-postal we'd take right now — you with your arm round me.

DAN [*bounces up*]. The Lord stand between me and the snares o' Satan, amen!

DAISY. What's the trouble, Den?

DAN. I'm a dacent boy — that's the trouble!

DAISY. But, Den, we gotta get married, or your dad'll be so mad.

DAN [*retreats and is followed by* DAISY]. That's nice

talk — about marriage — afore you know me five
minutes. . . . Keep back now. Don't surround
me.

DAISY. You ain't skeert, Den, are you?

DAN. Oh, I can defend myself. . . . Keep back!
Don't swarm in on me. [*Moves backwards.*]

DAISY [*following him*]. Why are you backing your
cart thataways? Why not halt and talk?

DAN [*warding her off*]. Don't crowd me now.
Keep a civil distance. . . . [*Moves on.*]

DAISY. Now, Denny, you know in your heart you
just love your own Daisy. Ain't it so? Mind, I
ain't a gel to chase a man around.

DAN. Back, back, back! [*Picks up shovel.*]

DAISY [*halts*]. Look at here, young man. Are we
going to make a contract, yea or nay? Now, speak.

DAN. No contracts, no contracts. I'm not a
marryin' man.

DAISY. Then I guess that settles it. Let's tell
dad. [*She goes towards room door.*]

DAN. Hi, wait a minute. [*Scratching his head*]
That would be twartin' him.

DAISY [*comes back*]. How now, Denny? Changed
your mind, have you?

DAN [*feebly*]. I dunno what to say. . . . God help
me, amen.

DAISY [*taking his arm*]. Let's sit down, Denny,
and I'll tell you what to do. [*They sit.*] This, you
understand, ain't no boy-and-gel love-affair. No,
sir: this is a deal. Your dad has seen my papers
and they suit him. He needs my money to finish
this house, and you can't have the dollars without
Daisy. [*Draws closer.*] Now, Den, it's your move.
Don't be skeert to offend me. . . .

DENIS M'GOTHIGAN *and* ROSE *come in.* DENIS *is a sturdy little man with a beard.*

DENIS. Well, are ye foolin' another gerril, Dan? Is't not enough to fool my daughter without foolin' the whole naborhood?

DAN [*jumps up*]. I'm in flames, but this is a judgement! [*Gazing blankly at* DENIS] My fader's in the room, Denis. If he comes out he'll martyr me.

DENIS. Oh, the sooner he hears my business the better. [*Shouts.*] I've no cows grazed with James Deegan, LL.D. I disregard the ould lan'grabber or the breed of him.

DEEGAN *comes in.*

DAN [*wringing his hands*]. I wish the ground would open its mouth and swally me!

DEEGAN. Small farmers have loud voices. Whom are you threatening now, Denis?

DENIS. I'm come to see about this match between your fool son and my daughter. I didn't seek the match, nor help to make it. But the job's done now, and I'll make him abide by it. He'll not make a laughin'-stock of my daughter. [*Stamps his foot.*] I'm damned if he will!

DEEGAN. Have you anything in writing, Denis?

DENIS. No, but I've an eye-witness. Paul Twyning seen and heard the whole business. . . .

PAUL *comes in, back.*

PAUL. Who's taking my name in vain? Paul Twyning's a stranger in your midst and won't have his name mixed up in any rural squabble. . . .

DAN. That's right, Paul. Deny everything.

DENIS [*hotly to* PAUL]. Ye were an eye-witness! D'ye hear? [*Menacing* PAUL] If ye deny it, I'll smash ye!

PAUL [*flies off the handle*]. Roast the mongrel in the nine counties of Ulster can put them up to Paul Twyning! [*Squaring up*] Come on now — the whole lot of you! [*Knocks the hat off* DENIS.] Come on, I say! For three weeks in this barren land has left me blue-mouldin' for a fight. . . .

DEEGAN. Order! I'll not have my house turned into a Dublin doss-house.

DAN. That's right, fader. You know the law.

DEEGAN [*cuffs* DAN]. How dare you speak, sir! I'll take the belt to you later.

DAN. God help me, amen. I'm always blamed.

DEEGAN. Denis M'Gothigan, promise or no promise, you've no case. My prodigal boy has nothing here but the name.

DENIS. Oh, we'll see all about that. The prodigal can claim for sarvant's wages. [*Stamps his foot.*] By the holy, you'll not twist Denis. . . . I've an eye-witness and a ring and a conversation-lozenger.

DAN. It's a lie!

DENIS. Here, gerril: hand me that lozenger. [ROSE *gives him an outsize in them.*] Wait till the jury hears this. [*Reads:*]

> " I love you very dearly,
>   And if you love me,
>   In spite of wind and weather
>   We shall married be."

DAN. It's a lie! I never had that lozenger in my possession. 'Twas a wee peppermint I give her.

ROSE. Oh, Dan, Dan!

I

DAN. Oh, it's easy for you to " Dan, Dan ". But it's me's fightin' for my life.

ROSE. And there's the ring. [*Holds it up.*]

DAN. That's not my ring at all. It's Paul Twyning's ring. He picked it up — or stole it from the pilgrims — at Lisdoonvarna.

PAUL. Dan Deegan, mind what you're saying, or you'll have a slander case on your hands. . . .

DAN. I know rightly what I'm saying. I'm in flames, but I mean to clear myself!

DEEGAN. Denis M'Gothigan, the courts are open to you. But I think it my duty to inform you that this boy is about to emigrate. . . .

DAN [*bursts into tears*]. A bad end to you, Paul Twyning! This is what comes of bad company. I was a happy boy till I met you. [*Sobs bitterly.*]

PAUL. The prayers of the wicked have no travalley. You've gone the pace, Dan, and you must take the consequences.

ROSE [*whimpering*]. Don't emigrate him, Mr. Deegan. I don't care about myself . . . but don't emigrate Dan.

DENIS [*grabs* ROSE]. Come on, m'gerril! I'll have none of your whumpering. I'll have damages, or I'll rid the country of him. [*He leads* ROSE *out.*]

PAUL. You'll be another Columcille, Dan. You won't even get back to Ireland blindfolded. [*Looks about the floor.*] Well, begorry after I searching the whole place, outside and in, there is my spatula. [*Picks it up and goes to the room.*]

DEEGAN [*roars at* DAN]. Go and take off your good clothes — you damned prodigal scoundrel, you!

DAN *goes into the room blubbering.*

DAISY [*rising*]. Mr. Deegan, I feel downright sorry for you, I do.

DEEGAN. I'm obliged to you, Miss Mullan. But this is not my first trouble of the kind. I had to banish four other sons and two daughters for disobedience, and this boy is by far the worst of the lot.

DAISY. It's a plum shame the way your family have treated you. Here you are with a new house and a big farm, and nobody to look after you but a few servants. It's a downright crime. [*The room door is opened cautiously and* DAN *is seen listening.*] Why, my dear friend, what you want is a kind-hearted young woman to look after you and take an interest in you.

DEEGAN. I wish I'd thought of that twenty years ago. I'm too old now.

DAISY. Too old! Why, you're a fresher-looking man than your son Den. In America a man of your age is dancing and flirting and only beginning to enjoy life.

DEEGAN. It's good of you to flatter an old man. [*Lays his hand on her shoulder.*] If I'd met you fifteen or twenty years ago, I might have put a certain question to you.

DAISY. If you'd met me even ten years ago, you'd have met a comparatively poor gel, for I've made all my money in the last decade. But ain't it better late then never?

DEEGAN [*animated*]. Mind what you're saying, Daisy. My heart is younger than my face.

DAISY. I know fine what I'm saying, Jimes. And I repeat — ain't it better late than never?

DEEGAN. You'd give me a new lease of life.

DAISY. I sure would, dear.

DEEGAN. I'm not after your money, Daisy. I'd make you an assignment of everything I possess in the world.

DAISY. And I'd take care you wanted for nothing. I'd have your house and garden the talk of this here settlement. Out there in front of the door I'd have a double hedge of sweet-pea. . . .

DEEGAN [*drops on one knee and takes her hand*]. Daisy, without further debate, will you marry me?

DAN [*shouts*]. Paul, Paul! The ould man's down on his knees. . . . Good God! the man that shook hands wi' Parnell himself. . . .

PAUL [*dashes in*]. Congratulations! Congratulations! Is it all settled?

DAISY. Why, sure it is. He's asked me to marry him, and my answer is — Yaas.

PAUL. And if you ever want a witness — I'll be here. [*Going*] And ten to one I'll be called.

Curtain

ACT II

A drinking-room in PATRICK DEEGAN's *public-house, the following day. There is a door to the kitchen, one to the bar, and a side-door to the yard.*

PATRICK, *a big, coarse man of unteetotal aspect, comes in from the bar, followed by* PAUL *and* DAN.

PAT. Now don't all spake at once. Let Paul Twyning, that has travelled the world and seen something in his time, tell me about this calamity. One thing we all know: if Daisy Mullan had the ould man on his knees, she never let him up till he settled the business.

MRS. DEEGAN, *a grey-haired woman with a troubled face, looks in from the bar.*

MRS. DEEGAN. Patrick, dear, won't you let me come in and hear the rest of it.

PAT. Away to blazes, you, and mind the bar! If I want your advice I'll send for you. I never had an hour's luck since the day I tane you.

MRS. DEEGAN. Well, well. You'll maybe get rid of me, then you'll have good luck. [*She turns to go.*]

PAT. Here! bring us something to drink. What's yours, Paul?

PAUL. Plain whiskey for me.

DAN. Me a spoonful o' wine.

PAT. Wine the devil! [*To* MRS. DEEGAN] Three glasses of whiskey from the wee jar in the gas-meter. Hurry!

MRS. DEEGAN [*comes back*]. Patrick Deegan, are

you wild mad? If you taste whiskey this day and your father coming in — I know what'll happen. He'll sign this house over to Daisy Mullan, and we'll be left homeless.

PAT. Shut your long face and bring the whiskey! Could I do business without a good rosiner to steady me? Fly now!

MRS. DEEGAN. Oh, very well. You'll see who's right, and who's wrong, before the chapel bell rings six. [*She goes to the bar.*]

PAT. Take sates, boys. I can't sit down, I'm that put about.

PAUL *and* DAN *sit at table.* MRS. DEEGAN *comes in with three glasses on a tray.*

PAUL. Here's that the hinges of friendship may never rust . . .

PAT. Don't drink a minute, Paul. I want to ask you one question. Are you on our side or the ould man's? Mind, a five-pound note never raired Pat Deegan. If you help me to manœuvre him into making me an assignment of this house — I'll not forget a friend.

PAUL. On principle I'm against the ould man.

PAT. Good, by Moses! On what principle, Paul?

PAUL. Moral and religious. That a man of seventy-five should be thinking about his sowl instead of his honeymoon.

PAT. A new proverb, by Moses! We'll drink to that afore we say another word. [*Raising his glass*] Here's a plague on ould Yankee Mullan! that has brought all this trouble on quiet, dacent people. [*All drink.*]

MRS. DEEGAN. Patrick, dear, Jim's in the bar.

Won't you let me stay and hear what you're going
to do?

PAT. Ay, surely to God! Who has a better right
to hear the outs and ins of it than my own Janey?
Sit down. [*She sits.*] Now, Paul, you're the man
I want to hear. What's your opinion of the whole
tragedy?

PAUL. Well, in the first place, I think your father
— God forgive him! — has treated his fine family
worse than the mud on the road. Four sons and
two daughters banished, the boy Dan about to be
pushed out with the grey ribs in his hair, and yourself a cottier with no more fixity of tenure than one
of Clanricarde's tenants in the evil days.

PAT [*grabs* MRS. DEEGAN'S *arm*]. D'ye hear that?
D'ye hear what a smart man that has paraded the
world says? Is them my own words a-fifty times over?

MRS. DEEGAN. Oh, many a time you said that,
Patrick.

PAT. Purceed, Paul.

PAUL. And the worst — the saddest feature of all
— James Deegan is an able man.

PAT. Able! A man that shook hands with
Parnell himself. A man that addressed the gowned
judges in the Four Coorts. Ay, by Moses, he's an
able man!

PAUL. But, like every great man of ancient or
modern times, James Deegan has made a mess in
the last lap.

PAT. Ay, look at Parnell himself!

PAUL. I almost despair of human nature when I
see James Deegan — a white-haired man, as grave
and solemn as a Pilgrim Father — making love on
his two knees to an ould washed-out Yankee cook.

PAT. By Moses, no wonder you despair.

MRS. DEEGAN. Now, you'll blether on till he comes in. Then you'll have less to say.

PAUL. The lady is right. He'll be in soon, for we passed him and his fiancée in the trap within a mile of the town. Myself and Dan were in a creamery waggon, and we covered up with empty sacks that he wouldn't see us.

MRS. DEEGAN. In God's name, will Daisy Mullan marry him?

PAUL. Would a duck swallow a dew-worm?

MRS. DEEGAN. Has she property in America?

PAUL. I don't know about the property, but she's more documents in her vanity-bag than the Congested Districts Boord. And she'll have more before night, for he'll sign the farm over to her this day in front of an attorney.

PAT. Oh, my head, my head! [*Holds his head.*] By Moses, I'm dizzy!

MRS. DEEGAN. Dan, if she wants a man, why didn't you take her yourself?

PAUL. Poor Dan has his own troubles. Isn't he pledged to Rose M'Gothigan?

PAT. What! Pledged to who?

PAUL. Now, for pity's sake, don't attack Dan. How could he be wise and his father a fool? He'd the misfortune to speak to Rose and she consented.

PAT [*reaching for* DAN]. For a farden I'd tear out the win'pipe! I see it all now. You were sitting humpt up beside her the whole night of the dance. . . . It's you has riz the devil in the ould man. [*Reaches out again.*] I'll tear out the win'pipe. . . .

DAN. Don't touch me now! I'm in flames, if I'll stand it.

PAUL. Leave Dan alone, Patrick. Isn't he well enough punished, and he about to be shipped to foreign parts?

JIM, *a thin boy of eighteen, comes in from the bar.*

JIM. I say, I say! My granda's away driving up the street with a woman in the trap.

PAT. Did he not stop at the door?

JIM. He never looked in as much as.

PAUL. He's taking Daisy up to the bank. She's got a Yankee draft, and he's going to endorse it.

PAT. He'll rue that, by Moses! I never seen a Yankee draft yet worth tuppence. [*To* JIM] Away you out to the bar. . . . G'on, afore I lift something and split your skull.

JIM. What's wrong, da?

PAT. Away, and don't ask so many questions. You'd talk as much as your mother. . . . Away, afore I lift something and brain you!

JIM. Is my granda going to marry that woman, da?

PAT. Ay, he wants a wife instead of a coffin. Go on now, like a good son, and mind the bar. That's a good boy.

JIM. And will he not lay me the farm — and me called for him?

DAN. Flames, what right have you to the farm?

JIM. Da, won't you? . . .

PAT. Will you go and mind the bar? [*Makes a race at him.*] By Moses, I'll lame ye! [JIM *runs out.*] Your mother has you spoiled.

PAUL [*rising*]. I don't want the ould man to see me here at all, for he left me plastering the parlour room. . . . I'll sit in the kitchen and sip a bottle of stout. Come on, Dan. [*He and* DAN *go out.*]

PAT. This is a tragedy! Daisy Mullan'll revenge herself on me. . . .

MRS. DEEGAN [*rising*]. What for? What has Daisy Mullan against you?

PAT. I coorted her a while about thirty years ago.♪

MRS. DEEGAN. Oh, she was lucky she didn't get you. She'll know that when she sees you.

PAT [*looks wild*]. I'll go and get blind drunk!

MRS. DEEGAN. You'll do nothing of the kind. You'll leave everything to me. Who knows but this is all for good? If he ships Dan, we might be able to stop the wedding, and then Jim would get the farm and everything.

PAT. If you manage that, I'll buy you the best pair o' slippers in Ballybullion. I will, by Moses!

JIM *rushes in.*

JIM. I say, I say! My granda's away into the yard. The woman's in the bank. And Denis M'Gothigan and his daughter Rose is away into Attorney Dawson's. . . .

MRS. DEEGAN. Well, well! one thing at once. You're like all the Deegans — you won't make it any smaller. [*To* PAT] Go out and help your father to put in the mare, and don't let on you know a ha'porth.

PAT. I'll be as nice as ninepence at first. But if he doesn't sign this place over to me this day, I'll give him and ould Daisy a weddin' present, by Moses! [*Goes out side-door to yard.*]

JIM. Ma, what's wrong?

MRS. DEEGAN. Don't bother me, son.

JIM. My granda looks powerful stern.

MRS. DEEGAN. Well, be you very glad to see him when he comes in, and remind him that you're called for him.

JIM. Heth, I will, ma. But if he doesn't lay me the farm or gimme money, I'll tell him another story some day!

MRS. DEEGAN [*with energy*]. Listen to me. Take the wee bottle and sixpence, and tell the druggist to fill it for your ma. And don't let anybody see what you're getting. Just slip the bottle to himself; he knows what I want.

JIM. All right, ma. [*Goes out.*]

MRS. DEEGAN. He may sign the farm, but he won't sign this house to Daisy Mullan. . . . The old viper! what does he want with a woman. . . .

DEEGAN *comes in at side-door. He has a whip and a rug and is looking very spry.*

DEEGAN. Well, how's all here?

MRS. DEEGAN [*fussing*]. Och, granda dear, is this yourself! [*Shakes hands and laughs.*] Upon my word, granda, you're looking fresher every day.

DEEGAN. I'm like the eagles, I'm renewing my youth. [*Lays down whip and rug and sits at table.*]

MRS. DEEGAN. It's nothing short of a miracle — at your great age. I suppose you're hard on eighty.

DEEGAN. A man is just as old as he feels. I feel about twenty-five.

JIM *rushes in and slips the bottle to his mother.*

JIM. Och, is this my wee granda!

MRS. DEEGAN. Yes, you'll be happy now. You've been wishing and wishing your granda would come in.

JIM. Och, my dear granda! [*Hugs him.*] My own dear granda that I'm called for. Amn't I, granda? Amn't I your favourite grandchild?

DEEGAN [*gives him a penny*]. There's a penny for yourself. Go and buy liquorice-ball.

JIM. Och, it takes yourself, granda! [*Tries to kiss him.*] You'll lay me more than a penny some day. Won't you, granda?

DEEGAN. I'll see. Go now and buy liquorice-ball. You're getting too old for this baby-talk.

JIM. It's because I love my granda. [*Goes out with hanging head.*]

MRS. DEEGAN. You shouldn't cut him, granda. He's that doted on you.

DEEGAN. He's like all the rest, he's doted on my last will and testament.

MRS. DEEGAN. May God forgive you, James Deegan, for thinking such a thing, let alone to say it.

DEEGAN [*shrugs*]. We won't further discuss it. . . . Have you seen Daniel?

MRS. DEEGAN. I think he's about the house somewhere.

DEEGAN. I presume he has emptied his stomach?

MRS. DEEGAN. Och, he was talking as usual, but I was busy and paid no attention. Poor Dan has always a long story about your cruelty, but I seldom listen to it.

DEEGAN. You're a wise woman — and a rare woman — to pay no attention to stories. Send Daniel to me: he's in the kitchen.

MRS. DEEGAN. Och, granda, won't you take something after the drive?

DEEGAN. Not at present. I have important legal

business to transact, and I make it a rule to keep the head clear for business. Tell Daniel to come forth.

MRS. DEEGAN. You were always a great business man, granda. I wish your sons had taken after you.

DEEGAN. My sons were graceless and without understanding. Send Daniel to me.

MRS. DEEGAN *goes to the kitchen and* PAT *comes in side-door.*

PAT. I tell you, father, that mare's in big fettle. But she needs a bit off her mane and tail.

DEEGAN. Her mane and tail will do very well. But what about yourself? You've had another spill since I was here.

PAT [*lamely*]. It was the fair day, and I got a half 'un too much. But I've tane the pledge for life. . . .

DEEGAN. Silence, sir! How dare you add falsehood to iniquity? The pledge for life! Couldn't I smell your breath the moment I entered the yard?

PAT. Ay, that's right — I tane a thim'leful this morning.

DEEGAN. Patrick Deegan, beware! I may have to answer at the Bar of Judgement for putting you in a tavern. Take this from me as final. One other burst and I'll put this property to the hammer.

PAT. I could curse the day you ever put me in it.

DEEGAN. And I've been cursing the day ever since.

PAT. If you'd gimme the property at first and let me run it in my own way, I'd be a different man to-day.

DEEGAN. A different man, indeed! You'd be in the grave or the madhouse. [*Stands up.*] Since you've raised the question I'll settle it now, once for all.   Then you'll know where you are.

PAT. That's all I want to know.

DEEGAN. Your name will never be written in the deed of this property.   Now you know.

PAT. Say that again!

DEEGAN. If I don't sell the house I'll leave it to your crafty wife, and she in turn will leave it to her crafty son.   Now, sir.   That's your settlement. [*Sits down.*]

PAT. The day you do that I'll burn it to ashes! I will, by Moses!

DEEGAN. And welcome.   It's well insured.

PAT [*boils over*]. Ay, maybe it is! maybe it's well insured.   I know nothing about it, I'm only the tenant.   But I know this: you'd better insure yourself.   D'ye hear?   Insure yourself and the ould Yankee trooper. . . .

DAISY *comes in from bar, her face flaming.*

DAISY. Patrick Deegan, who are you calling names!   Me, is it?   I'm the old Yankee trooper, am I?

PAT. Shut up!   Shut up — or I'll shoot ye out to the middle of the street!

MRS. DEEGAN *rushes in.*

MRS. DEEGAN. What's wrong?   What on earth is wrong?

DAISY. James Deegan, am I to be treated in this low-down manner, am I?   Is this how you mean to protect me as your wife, is it?

DEEGAN [*stands up*]. Patrick Deegan, you've done a bad day's work for yourself and for those who come after you.

PAT [*wildly*]. Ah, shut up, you! You're the great man that shook hands with Parnell himself! You're the great lawyer that addressed the gowned judges in the Four Coorts! And here you are at last — tane up wi' an ould Yankee scullion! [MRS. DEEGAN *grabs hold of* PAT *and drags him out, he shouting*] Ould Yankee trooper. . . . Ould scullion. . . . Ould mazawatty! [*She gets him dragged out to the bar.*]

DAISY. Jimes, these folks don't want me. That woman just hates me like a snake. See the cold look in her eyes, and the snarl on her lip like a wolf. [*Sits down.*]

DEEGAN. She may snarl, but she can't bite. Before we leave the town you'll be her landlady.

DAISY. Oh, Jimes, how good you are to me. [*Looks round.*] And you bet I'll see they keep this place in order.

MRS. DEEGAN *comes in with two drinks on a tray.*

MRS. DEEGAN. Granda, dear, you know what Patrick is. He's that hasty. [*To* DAISY] My dear, he wouldn't hurt your feelings for the world. [*Laughs dryly.*] Och, sure, from what I hear, you'll soon be one of the family.

DAISY. Yeah! and a nice family reception I'm gittin'. An old Yankee trooper, no less!

MRS. DEEGAN. Och, nobody heeds Pat Deegan. I wish you both many happy days. I've something here to wet the match. A small special for you, granda, and a port for Miss Mullan.

DAISY. I sure want something after that racket. [*To* DEEGAN] Drink that up, dear; it'll do you good. [*Both drink.*]

MRS. DEEGAN. I hope you'll give us the big day soon. [*Picks up tray.*] I'll leave you now. As the saying is, three's a crowd. [*She goes out.*]

DAISY. That's a cruel woman, Jimes. Ain't she, dear?

DEEGAN. A crafty lady. You had no trouble at the bank.

DAISY. Why, no. The manager, a real nice man, just glanced at your endorsement and smiled pleasant. [*Opens bag.*] I got the whole wad right here. [*Shows him roll of notes.*]

DEEGAN. That's too much money to carry on your person. You should have left it — or part of it — in the bank.

DAISY. No, sir. I'm putting every cent of this into our new home, for nice furniture and nifty wall-paper and carpets. [*Puts it back in the bag.*] I told you I was going to make you comfortable, and you bet I am.

JIM *rushes in.*

JIM. Och, my new grandma! My nice Yankee grandma. [*Tries to hug her.*]

DAISY [*pushing him away*]. Who the Helen Maria are you! [*Stands up.*]

JIM. Och, don't you know me? I'm called for my granda. . . . Amn't I, granda? Amn't I your favourite grandchild?

DAISY. Go on — beat it. You're too darned sweet to be wholesome.

JIM. Oh, wait till you know me, grandma——

DAISY. Go on — git! We can spare you. Skidoo. [*Sits.*]

DEEGAN. Where is Uncle Daniel, boy?

JIM. Him and Paul Twyning's in the kitchen, drinking mulled porter.

DEEGAN. Oh! has Paul followed the scent?

DAISY. What do you know about that? And we left him plastering the room.

JIM. Him and Uncle Dan came in the creamery waggon — covered with empty bags that you couldn't see them. They passed you on the road.

DEEGAN. Send them both to me.

JIM. Heth, I will. It's nice to be doing errands for my dear granda. [*Goes to the kitchen.*]

DAISY. Say, that's a fearful obnoxious kid, ain't he?

DEEGAN. The mother puts him up to it.

PAUL *staggers in, followed by* DAN.

PAUL. Here we are again, as large as life. And whoever doesn't like my gait needn't swing on it.

DEEGAN. Twyning, what are you doing here?

PAUL. Deegan, I'm waiting for a train to carry me home to Dublin town. [*Sings:*]

" For the ship went down with that fair
        young bride,
    That sailed from Dooooooooblin Bay."

DEEGAN. You're drunk, sir.

PAUL. Not yet. I'm only at the musical stage. [*Sings:*]

" In a pair of brand new brogues
    I rattled o'er the bogs,
    And frightened all the dogs
    On the rocky road to Dublin.
    . . . Tearing away, my boys——"

K

DEEGAN. Silence, sir!

PAUL. Silent, O Moyle, be the roar of thy waters.

DEEGAN. Aren't you going back to finish the plastering?

PAUL. Emphatically never. And I'll tell you why. I won't have my name appearing in morbid breach of promise cases. Is that emphatic? [*Takes the spatula from his pocket.*] I've my tools all here. [*Sings:*]

> " I'm bidding you a long farewell,
>   My Mary, kind and true. . . ."

DEEGAN. Be quiet, sir!

PAUL. Well, without setting it to music, I'm quit.

DAN. I'm in flames, but I'm going too! I can go wi' Paul and be his attender.

DEEGAN [*stands up*]. What is that you say?

DAN [*cowering*]. Nothing, fader.

DEEGAN. Come with me, sir. [*Walks unsteadily toward the door.*]

DAN. The emigration agent!

DEEGAN [*stops*]. My head feels somewhat light.

DAISY. Same here, Jimes. [*Her hat tilts on one side.*] A sort of dopey feeling.

DEEGAN [*returns to his chair*]. Something she put in the drink. . . .

PAT *brings in* MR. O'HAGAN.

PAT [*in a surly voice*]. Atturney Hagan to see you.

O'HAGAN. I was just setting out for your place, Mr. Deegan, when I heard you were in town. [*Shakes hands.*] Are you well?

DEEGAN. Quite well, thank you. What can I do for you?

O'HAGAN. Haven't you a son named Daniel?

DEEGAN. Unfortunately, I have.

O'HAGAN. Well, seems he's broken his promise to marry a Miss Rose M'Gothigan, a daughter of Denis's.

DAN. It's a lie! I never spoke to the girl in my life.

O'HAGAN. Oh, is this the boy himself? [*Smiles at* DAN.] The young lady tells a different story, Dan. She and her father are in the town looking for law.

DAN. Let them law away. I'm stainless. Get the prayer book and swear me.

O'HAGAN [*to* DEEGAN]. Denis M'Gothigan has a very strong case, sir. What are we going to do?

DEEGAN. Fight it.

DAN. That's right, fader. Fight it.

O'HAGAN. If you take my advice you'll give the girl a few pounds and settle it.

DAN. In God's name do, fader. Settle it. You never know what they might swear.

DEEGAN [*to* O'HAGAN]. This prodigal has nothing.

PAUL. He's a guilty conscience. I heard him with my own ears popping the question, and saw him with my own eyes putting the ring on her finger. If that isn't a clear case for the plaintiff, I'll eat my spatula.

O'HAGAN. You hear that, Mr. Deegan. You're not mad enough to fight a case like that. [*He whispers to* PAT, *who goes out to the bar.*] We must settle it, James. We've no case.

DAISY [*in a sleepy voice*]. Se'l it, dear, se'l it. We don't want no law-suits.

PAT *brings in* DENIS *and* ROSE.

o'HAGAN. Now, Denis, between ourselves, you've no case. But Mr. Deegan doesn't want to strive with a good neighbour.

DENIS. Ho! Is this the Four Coorts?

o'HAGAN. It's well for you it isn't the Four Courts. . . .

DENIS. Whisht! If we've no case we needn't waste your precious time. [*Takes* ROSE *by the hand.*] Come on, gerril. The Lord Chancellor O'Hagan says we've no case. That ring on your finger and the conversation lozenger in your pocket is sadly again us. [*Leads* ROSE *to the door.*]

o'HAGAN. Come back, Denis. It's my opinion you don't want a settlement. But you must be saved from yourself. Dan Deegan is a man of straw, but his father is ready to consider your terms.

DENIS [*leads* ROSE *back*]. That's a lash better than havin' no case at all.

o'HAGAN. Now, don't be too sarcastic. If we reach a settlement there must be no bitterness afterwards.

DENIS. I'm not a bitter man if I get fair play. Now make your offer.

o'HAGAN. We're prepared, without prejudice, to offer your daughter five pounds.

DENIS. Yaha! Yaha! Five pound for a good breach o' promise case! Come on, Rose. I can buy ye a new apron without damages. . . .

o'HAGAN. Then say it yourself.

DENIS. Without prejudice, three hunhert pound in goold. Now, sir!

o'HAGAN. No jury would give you more than ten pounds, and then you couldn't get a penny from Dan.

DENIS. I could rid the country of him.

DEEGAN. I'll do that without you. I'm shipping him myself.

DAN [*sobbing*]. I don't want to crass the seas. I'm too ould and I'm no skolard.

DENIS. You're not too ould to run after young gerrils. You and your conversation lozengers is a danger to the parish.

DAN [*weeping*]. Don't paint me blacker than I am, Denis. I never was a bad boy. [*Sobs quietly.*]

O'HAGAN. This is a very pathetic case. The poor lad doesn't want to leave the green hills and dales of holy Ireland.

DENIS. He should lave the gerrils alone.

O'HAGAN. Ah, shame, Denis! You were young yourself. Any Irish jury would forgive Dan for passing a lozenger to lovely Rose M'Gothigan. [*To* ROSE] I'll engage you wouldn't like to see your Willy Reilly banished — would you, now?

ROSE. No, indeed, sir. [*Sniffs.*] It's not me that's driving him across the seas.

DAN. God bliss you, Rose. Amen.

DENIS. Be quiet, gerril! I'll have no more of this soapy nonsense. I know what O'Hagan's flowery talk amounts to.

PAUL [*rising*]. Let Paul Twyning speak a word. The solution of this problem is as plain as the nose on your face. Let James Deegan and Denis M'Gothigan give the lovers a modest start in life— sure, the costs of a Dublin law-suit would do it.

DENIS. I'm game. I'm raisonable.

O'HAGAN. Now, Mr. Deegan, what do you say?

DEEGAN. If one penny of my money would buy them a freehold I wouldn't give it.

PAUL [*hotly*]. No, bedamned to you for a pigheaded, selfish ould slave-driver! You'd sooner put them aboord the emigrant ship.

O'HAGAN. Oh, this is going too far.

DEEGAN. Not at all. Let the vagrant have his say.

PAUL. And the vagrant *will* have his say. Ireland, north, south, east, and west, is lousy with your kind. There was more happiness on the Irish homestead when you were paying the rack-rent and eating the lumpers.

PAT. Smite him, Paul! Smite him!

PAUL. The omnipotent God only knows what you'll be like if you ever get Home Rule. I wouldn't like to be Dan Deegan and vote for Labour.

DEEGAN. Whatever rule we may have, we'll always have our tramps and paupers.

PAUL. And your Dans! who are more destitute than any paupers I've met. [*Points to* DAN] Just look at that product of yourself and ninety-five acres of Irish soil. No more spine than a lizard, and so bulldozed and brow-beaten that he'd swear a lie before he'd own the simplest truth.

DAN. I never tould the truth in my life.

PAUL. Standing there, with grey head and shaking limbs, you'd think he'd killed somebody instead of given a lozenger to Rose M'Gothigan. [*Loudly*] And Dan Deegan is legion. And ould Deegan is legion. You drive the youth to the four winds, and then bleat and pray and send them shamrocks in exile. . . . Ah, gimme a drink, somebody.

PAT. Come on wi' me, Paul! By Moses, you're as powerful as Paul and the Corinthians. [*He lugs* PAUL *out to the bar.*]

DEEGAN. There's a Labour leader lost in that frothy scoundrel.

o'HAGAN. It's not all froth, what he says. . . . Denis, you were amenable up to a point. Now, what's the lowest figure you could accept?

DENIS. Three hunhert pound — in goold.

o'HAGAN. I see. [*To* DEEGAN] How far are you prepared to meet him?

DEEGAN. A single penny of mine will never rattle in a M'Gothigan's pocket.

DENIS. Come on, Rose. We'll see the Four Coorts, after all.

ROSE. Good-bye, Dan.

DAN. Good-bye, Rose. I was a happy boy till I met you.

DENIS. Come on, gerril. [*He and* ROSE *go out.*]

DEEGAN [*to* DAN]. Step outside, sir. I want to speak to Mr. O'Hagan.

DAN. Yes, fader. [*Goes out.*]

DAISY. Jimes, I feel awful sleepy and queerish. I believe that wine was doped——

DEEGAN. I'm sure of it. My own feet and legs are tingling, but the mind is clear.

MRS. DEEGAN *comes in.*

MRS. DEEGAN. You'll take a cup of tea, granda.

DEEGAN. I want first to know what you put in my glass?

MRS. DEEGAN. Granda! such a question to ask me. It was a fresh bottle——

DEEGAN. That will do. I've heard drug stories about this house; now I'm convinced.

DAISY. You sure put something in mine, dope or something. I can't keep my eyes awake.

MRS. DEEGAN. Ach, you're beside yourselves, the two of you! [*Goes out.*]

DEEGAN. Mr. O'Hagan, this lady, Miss Mullan, and I've arranged to get married. She has considerable property in America, and I want to make her an assignment of these licensed premises and the farm.

O'HAGAN. As from your marriage day?

DEEGAN. Exactly so.

O'HAGAN [*shaking hands*]. Congratulations, Miss Mullan.

DAISY. Thank you. I guess I'll want a good smart lawyer to look after my interests in America.

O'HAGAN [*bowing*]. Your husband will be able to bring you to the right man. [*To* DEEGAN] You want this matter arranged to-day, Mr. Deegan?

DEEGAN. Immediately. Then the M'Gothigans can proceed with their writs.

O'HAGAN. Splendid! You didn't attend the Four Courts for nothing.

DAISY. Ain't he just a dandy? I'm sure proud of my fiancé.

O'HAGAN. I'll have the document ready rightaway. Will you come over to the office and sign it?

DEEGAN. If I'm not there when it's ready, bring it over here.

O'HAGAN. With pleasure. [*Goes out.*]

DAISY. Jimes, dear, we must coax Paul Twyning to come back and finish the plastering, else our marriage will be held up for weeks.

DEEGAN. I've thought of that. We must get the ruffian back. [*He touches a small bell on table and* JIM *rushes in.*]

JIM. Och, does my granda want me! [*Tries to kiss him.*] You're not angry at me now, granda?

DAISY. Give him a keek, Jimes! Gee, he makes

me hot! Look ahyar, slobber! You get your message and beat it.

JIM. It's a great sin for you to put in between granda and his favourite grandchild.

DAISY. If I could get up I'd fetch you one!

DEEGAN. Be off, boy! Send Paul Twyning to me.

JIM [going]. Granda has turned clean again me. [Goes out.]

DAISY. Shucks! that boy gives me a bilious attack. I'd like to hitch him to a post and whale the everlasting daylights out of him.

PAUL staggers in.

PAUL [steadying himself]. " I sometimes wonder what the vintners buy one half so precious as the stuff they sell."

DEEGAN. Are you coming back to finish the plastering?

PAUL. The answer is in the negative.

DAISY. But I say y'are! And I'm going to make it worth your while. [She opens the bag.]

DEEGAN leans back and falls asleep.

PAUL. Of course, a request from a young bride-to-be puts a different complexion on it.

DAISY [takes out roll of money and hands him a pound note]. Thar's five dollars.

PAUL. With all due respect — this is a pound note.

DAISY. Yeah : five dollars. That's for you.

PAUL [bowing]. The strike is over. Work in all departments will commence to-morrow morning. [Pointing to DEEGAN] Is your fiancé asleep?

DAISY. I reckon he's dozing, and I'm just dying to. [Yawns.]

PAUL. Well, don't let me keep you awake. [*Goes to bar door and stands with knob in his hand.*]

DAISY [*yawning*]. Ah, yah, my . . . yaaaah. [*Leans back and sleeps.*]

PAUL [*slips over to them*]. Have you crossed the Rubicon? [*No answer.*] Do you not hear Cupid himself speaking to you? [*No answer.*] "Oh, take the cash and let the credit go, nor heed the rumble of a distant drum." [*He takes the roll of money and other papers from* DAISY's *bag and goes out the side-door.* MRS. DEEGAN *comes in, with tea on a tray.*]

MRS. DEEGAN. My goodness! [*Lays down tray.*] Wake up and take this cup of tea. [*No response. She glances nervously about the room, then goes through* DAISY's *bag and finds it empty.*] My goodness!

PAT *comes in from the bar.*

PAT. What's wrong here? Did you dose them?

MRS. DEEGAN. Not so loud—you fool!

PAT. 'Twould be no harm to see what ould Daisy has in the bag.

MRS. DEEGAN. For shame, man! Would you stoop to such a thing?

PAT. I'd stoop to anything this minute. Take away that tray. [MRS. DEEGAN *goes out with the tray, and* PAT *goes through the bag.*] Not a rupee, by Moses!

O'HAGAN, PAUL, *and* DAN *come in from the bar.*

O'HAGAN [*a document in his hand*]. What's the matter? Are they drunk or sleeping?

PAT. They're both. They killed a whole bottle between them.

MRS. DEEGAN *comes in*.

O'HAGAN. I want his signature to this paper.

MRS. DEEGAN. Granda's not in a fit condition to sign any paper.

PAT. Now, O'Hagan, I know and you know what's in that paper. You'd lay me on the street.

O'HAGAN. I can't help that, Patrick.

PAUL. Let me speak a word. Mr. O'Hagan, you live across the street, and many a bright pound Patrick Deegan has sent your way in the last twenty years. Is that right?

O'HAGAN. Quite true.

PAUL. And many another he could throw your way in the next twenty years.

O'HAGAN. That is so.

PAUL. I make bould to say you've no sympathy with your moribund client getting married on the edge of the grave and robbing his own childer?

O'HAGAN. I certainly don't think it's right.

PAUL. Then it's your duty to stop the match. Your duty to your client, to your neighbour, and to yourself. And Patrick Deegan will make it worth your while, both now and now-after.

PAT. Paul, I know you're a well-educated man, but I don't see what you're drivin' at.

PAUL. No, God help you altogether, you're a dull lot. Why, James Deegan, in a state of coma, will sign one paper as fast as another — if his hand is properly held, — and I suggest to you, Mr. O'Hagan, that we assign the farm to Dan and the pub to Patrick.

PAT [*grabbing his hand*]. My life on you, ould Dublin!

MRS. DEEGAN. Yes, Paul Twyning has a head on him. He's not all splutter and nonsense.

PAUL. Now, Mr. O'Hagan, what do you say to it? Deegan brothers will give you ten pounds apiece.

MRS. DEEGAN. Patrick will give twenty and Dan thirty.

PAUL. Fifty pounds, Mr. O'Hagan. No lawyer since the Stone Age ever refused fifty pounds.

O'HAGAN. Then I'll be the first to gain that distinction. I disapprove of James Deegan's plans, but that's his own affair. I won't sell my old client in his sleep.

DEEGAN [*yawns*]. Thank you, Mr. O'Hagan. You're your father's son.

PAUL. We were only trying to tempt him, but he's incorruptible. . . . God works wonders now and then: here stands a lawyer an honest man.

DEEGAN [*rubs his eyes*]. Do you want my signature, Mr. O'Hagan?

O'HAGAN. Yes, sir. This is ready. [*Takes out fountain pen.*]

DEEGAN. I'll sign in one moment. [*Rises unsteadily and shakes* DAISY.] Wake up! This is no place to fall asleep.

DAISY. Yeah . . . eh . . . what?

DEEGAN. Wake up. We're going home.

DAISY *sits up and arranges her hat.* DEEGAN *puts on his specs, scans the document, and signs it.*

DAISY [*screams*]. Oh, Jimes! Oh, gee! My money and papers — six hundred pounds — all gone! Stolen!

DEEGAN [*scans the faces about him; then to* DAISY].

Your money and papers are not far away. [*Looking hard at* PAT] Neither is the thief!

PAT *staggers against the wall, and* MRS. DEEGAN *faints on the floor.*

PAUL [*shouts*]. Water! water! And brandy for me!

Curtain

ACT III

The same as in Act I, three days later. It is evening.
PAUL *is mixing mortar on the floor.* ROSE *comes in with a small parcel in her hand.*

PAUL. Lord bless me, Rose, have you ventured in here again?

ROSE. Aren't the Deegans all away in the town?

PAUL. But they're due back at any minute.

ROSE. My father's in the town, too, and Daisy Mullan's visiting mother. She's crying sore about something. So I just come out.

PAUL. Daisy Mullan crying! I didn't think she'd a tear left in the cistern. She's maybe not as hard as she looks.

ROSE. She's crying bitter about something.

PAUL. Let's make a stagger at the cause. Wasn't there a young gentleman, not unlike a bank clerk, called on Daisy in the forenoon?

ROSE. Sure it was me seen him first. From the bank he was.

PAUL. Well, his visit might have something to do with Daisy's tears. The young banker called here and whispered something to ould Deegan, and it must have been something important, for ould Deegan turned as white as a sheet. Then he and the young banker drove off to town.

ROSE. And Dan's in the town buying his trunk.

PAUL. Dan's for Philadelphia in the morning . . . with his bundle on his shoulder.

ROSE [*offering parcel*]. Give Dan that when he comes in.   It's a muffler.

PAUL. Ah, let you wait and give it to him yourself. Sure, you'll see him before he takes the water.

ROSE. I may and I mayn't.   My father and me had a great battle last night, and I'm going to service.   Give Dan that, Paul, and tell him Rose wished him luck.

PAUL [*takes parcel*]. Well, well: the coorse of true love never runs smooth, and this is no exception.

ROSE. And good-bye to yourself, Paul.

PAUL [*takes her hand*]. Rose, I'm to blame for all this trouble.   I've risen a devil that I can't lay.

ROSE. Oh, don't say that, Paul.

PAUL. But I meant well.   The first time I limped up to your door you fed me and gimme a welcome change of socks.   And poor Dan gimme a left-foot boot, and said his father wanted a plasterer.

ROSE. Dan's kind.

PAUL. Kind but unstable.   I'd no sooner got this job than I commenced plotting a match between yourself and Dan; but, faith, I soon found that Dan was a shifty hero.

ROSE. He's afraid of his father.

PAUL. Afraid?   He lives in a state of mortal terror . . . like a young rabbit under the eye of a stoat.

ROSE [*freeing her hand*]. I must be going, Paul. If my father knew I was in here he'd kill me.

PAUL. Isn't your father in the town?

ROSE. He is.   He followed old Deegan, to see if he could find out what was wrong.

PAUL. It's not easy doing anything private in this locality. . . .

DAN *comes in. He is wearing a cheap new water-proof, a new hat, and carries a blackthorn and a tin trunk.*

ROSE. Dan!

PAUL. Willy Reilly himself!

DAN. No sconcing now, Paul Twyning! I'm in flames, if I'll suffer it. You're the means of gettin' me banished.

PAUL. I'll leave you now, Dan, for you're in a dangerous mood. [*Gives parcel to* ROSE.] You can deliver that yourself. [*He goes out, back.*]

ROSE. Maybe you wouldn't take this, Dan. It's a present.

DAN. Your father met me in the town and flew at me like a tager. . . . Hunted me into Pat's yard and affronted me.

ROSE. He's in a terrible pucker.

DAN. He vows he'll have my blood afore I put my fut on the boat.

ROSE. I'm going away, Dan. To service.

DAN. Ay, he blames me for that. You'll be well away, Rose. . . . I wish you were coming with me.

ROSE. I wish I was.

DAN. Across the ragin' main . . . the angry deep. The emigration agent says I'll make my fortune in six weeks . . . herdin' sheep in Philadelphy. Will you come, Rose — to the land of the settin' sun?

ROSE. Not now, Dan. But if you send for me——

DAN. I'm in flames, that's settled! I'll be as true as the stars above.

ROSE [*gives him parcel*]. It's only a muffler.

DAN. The very thing I wanted. I'll wear it on the deck, with the waves risin' mountains high, and I'll be thinkin' of you, Rose, and my native land. . . .

The angry voice of DENIS *is heard in the yard.*

ROSE. Oh, Dan, Dan! My father!

DAN. I'm in flames, but he'll murder us! . . . In here, Rose, in here! [*He and* ROSE *go into the cupboard.*]

PAUL *and* DENIS *come in.*

PAUL. I told you they weren't here, Denis. But you're that misdoubtful. Now, search the house.

DENIS. They're in here, I tell you. Somewhere in this house. If I get my thumb on Dan, I'll not lave much of him to go to America. I'll dismember him! [*Looks into the room.*] They're not in there.

PAUL. Nor they can't be upstairs, for the stairs are blocked.

DENIS. You'd try to smuggle them out if you could! But you won't fool Denis! I'll stand outbye and watch the house—if I stand for a week. [*He goes out.*]

PAUL [*speaking up to the ceiling*]. If you're upstairs, for heaven's sake lie low! Denis has got drink, and he wants blood.

DAISY *comes in.*

DAISY. Paul Twyning, I'm in a power of trouble, and I gotta talk to someone, or bust.

PAUL. Well — talk. It's more humane than the other. [*Points upstairs*] Not too loud, for Dan and Rose are hiding up there from Denis.

DAISY. Denis is waiting outside. He sure looks wild. But that ain't my trouble. I'm scared to pieces.

L

PAUL. What's frightened you?

DAISY [*glancing upward*]. They couldn't hear me up there, could they?

PAUL. Not if you stay in that key.

DAISY. I dunno how it is, but I got a hunch you're the sort of feller would stick to a gel in trouble.

PAUL. Go easy, now: I'm a plasterer myself.

DAISY. This ain't no josh. I'm waiting every minute to be arrested.

PAUL [*astonished*]. Taken into custody? A prisoner? For what?

DAISY [*breaks down*]. About that bank draft. 'Twas a fake. But I thought they wouldn't know for a few weeks, and that would gimme time to skip. But now they've spotted it.

PAUL. My sowl, this is a bad onion!

DAISY. It sure is. The bank manager sent for me and old Deegan, but I was too skeert to go in. [*Sobs.*] I just dunno what to do. . . .

PAUL. There's one thing you mustn't do in my presence — no weeping. For that would put me up the walls. [*Sits down beside her.*] And I want to help you. May I call you " Daisy ", just to comfort you?

DAISY. If you like. Sure you ain't married?

PAUL. No, glory be. I've been the whole seven kinds of galoot, but I'm still single.

DAISY. I sure want help.

PAUL. Well, dry your eyes. And don't wet them again, or I'll take to my heels.

DAISY [*dries her eyes*]. I'll try not to. But I'm sure in a hasp. I ain't no professional crook.

PAUL. That's plain, or you wouldn't break down over a trifle like this.

DAISY. I was trying to get even with old Deegan, but my plans miscarried and landed me in the wash.

PAUL. Were you going to marry old Deegan?

DAISY. No, seh! Not on your life. I wouldn't marry old Deegan — or his fool son — not if they owned the landscape.

PAUL. What, then, were you aiming at?

DAISY. I just meant to fix up a match, and then clear out with all I could rake up. But now the whole thing has gone flop, and I ain't got a nickel to meet that draft.

PAUL. That's unfortunate.

DAISY. Old Deegan thinks I still got that money, but I ain't. True to heaven, Paul Twyning, it was stolen in Pat Deegan's saloon. Patrick or his wife — or yon goat of a son — swiped the lot, papers and all.

PAUL. Were the papers valuable?

DAISY. They wasn't worth a cent. I was cook to a stockbroker, and my brother was janitor, and he got 'em in the trash basket.

PAUL. Waste paper?

DAISY. Sure. But my brother said if I flashed 'em round here I could marry some old guy with money.

PAUL. It's the pity your brother didn't come himself. He seems to've had the right idea.

DAISY. I wish he had come, or I hadn't.

PAUL. It's a great pity the law has power to step in and spoil the joke.

DAISY [*hands him a paper*]. My brother cooked up this cablegram. . . .

PAUL [*reads it*]. My sowl, your brother knows his business. He must be a partner in the firm of brokers. [*Returns it.*] Keep that like the sight of your eye. . . .

DAISY [*starts*]. I hear Deegan's car. [*Shaking.*] Oh, I can't face it. I'm all nerves.

PAUL. Listen to me, Daisy. Stiffen up and cut out them shivers. You've got all the decent cards in the pack, if you can play them.

DAISY. You think?

PAUL. I'm sure. Pay attention to me. Ould Deegan — the great lay lawyer — has made you an assignment of himself and his property. To get out of it he'll give you five or six hundred pounds.

DAISY. But the fake draft — how about it?

PAUL. Tell them it's a good draft. Tell them you paid your money for it in New York like a decent girl, and if it isn't in order the bank is to blame, not you.

DAISY. But my brother got it in the trash basket.

PAUL. The broad Atlantic is rowling between you and the trash basket. Follow my instructions and you'll win through.

The car is heard coming into the yard.

DAISY [*looks out*]. They're all here. . . . Patrick and Mrs. Deegan and O'Hagan. Paul, where can I go? I can't stay here.

PAUL. Go to the room, and listen carefully to the drift of our discoorse. I'll give a professional cough when I want you to come out. [DAISY *goes to room door.*] If O'Hagan asks you any impertinent questions, refer him to your American solicitors: Brown and FitzGerald, Broadway, New York. And if he wants a broker, refer him to Funk & Co., Wall Street.

DAISY. I hope he don't ask no questions. [*She goes to the room.*]

PAUL [*mixing mortar, sings:*]

" Daisy, Daisy, gimme your answer, do;
I'm half crazy all for the love of you.
It won't be a stylish marriage,
For we can't afford a carriage,
But you'll look nate upon the sate
Of a bicycle built for two."

DEEGAN, O'HAGAN, PAT, *and* MRS. DEEGAN *come in*.

PAT. Here's the tramp vagabone himself. We'll get the saddle on the right horse now, by Moses!

DEEGAN. Silence, sir, and let Mr. O'Hagan open the proceedings.

The table is brought to the centre and DEEGAN *and* O'HAGAN *sit down. The others stand.*

O'HAGAN [*opens attaché case*]. Twyning, we've proof that you took the money and papers from Miss Mullan's bag.

PAUL [*leans on the shovel*]. You've proof of that?

O'HAGAN. Yes, sir.

PAUL. You're very definite.

O'HAGAN. Yes, we're not here to mince matters. You stole the money, and we can prove it.

PAUL. Mr. O'Hagan, you can't bluff Paul Twyning. I've nothing to say.

O'HAGAN. Pat Deegan, what are you prepared to swear?

PAT [*excited*]. I can swear Paul Twyning left me in the bar, and went into the snug where my father and Daisy Mullan were asleep, and rifled the bag and slipped out the side-door.

PAUL. Was that why you staggered like a drunk cock and your wife fainted on the flure, when the whillabillo went up that the money was stolen?

O'HAGAN. Patrick has made a clean breast of it. He admits having examined the bag, as a precautionary measure, but found it empty.

DEEGAN. Patrick Deegan and his wife are not guilty. The sum was too large for them. Neither of them is honest, but they wouldn't have the nerve to steal six hundred pounds.

PAT [*raising his hand*]. May I fall dead if I lie! The bag was empty.

PAUL. Your intention was good, Patrick. Your father may think you wouldn't steal anything bigger than half a crown, but he's mistaken. The hand that opens a bag will take what's in it.

PAT. You took the money, Twyning! And I thinking with all your big speeches you were an honest man.

PAUL. An honest man should beware of going into your opium den.

O'HAGAN. This is all beside the point. Twyning, you were the only person that actually saw the roll of money. Miss Mullan gave you a pound note and put the rest in the bag. Is that right?

PAUL. Perfectly correct. I'd be sorry to deny receipt of a gift.

O'HAGAN. And you saw the roll of notes in her hand?

PAUL. Thank God, I'm not blind. I saw the rowl distinctly, and it as thick as my arm.

O'HAGAN. And you meant to catch the first train to Dublin, did you not?

PAUL. That was my intention. And that's where your case falls down. For if I'd annexed all that money, I wouldn't be here: I'd be sauntering down Grafton Street, with a cane in one hand and my suede gloves in the other.

PAT. You took it!

PAUL. Fancy a millionaire coming back here to plaster this duck-house at four bob a day! The thing's preposterous.

DEEGAN. Mr. O'Hagan, you are on the wrong track. I told you Paul Twyning was not the thief. I'm convinced that Daisy Mullan has the money and papers concealed. . . .

PAUL. Why should Daisy rob her own nest?

O'HAGAN [*rising*]. We'll go across to her own house and ask her. . . .

PAUL. You won't have to cross the wet grass. I think Miss Mullan is upstairs.

O'HAGAN. Ah, just what I feared! She and Twyning are both in it.

DEEGAN [*angrily*]. What is Daisy Mullan doing up my stairs?

PAUL. She said this was her own house, and what could I do? [*He coughs conspicuously and* DAISY *comes in.*]

DAISY. Quite a crowd here, ain't the'?

O'HAGAN. What were you doing up my client's stairs?

DAISY. Up whose stairs? Your client ain't got no stairs. This house is mine, stairs and all. See?

O'HAGAN. You'd better throw off that brazen cloak and realise where you stand. Your worthless draft has been discovered. You know what that means?

DAISY. Sure.   It means you folks don't know nuthin' about drafts.   Mine is O.K.

O'HAGAN. If it is you can have it back.   The bank doesn't want it.

DAISY. Neither do I.

O'HAGAN. The bank holds Mr. Deegan responsible for the money.   If you hand us the six hundred pounds we can settle with the bank, and avoid further trouble.   If you don't, Mr. Deegan can have you arrested.

DEEGAN. And I will.

DAISY. The money's somewhere in the Deegan family.   I sure ain't got it.   I was drugged and robbed in Patrick Deegan's awful den.   [*Flaring up.*]   What the heck do I care about the dab of money, compared with the loss of my deeds and documents!

O'HAGAN. Why were you carting all those valuable papers around with you?   Have you no lawyers?

DAISY. Can't I carry my own papers if I want to? But you'll know in a short time whether I've got lawyers or not.

O'HAGAN. The sooner the better.   Who are they?

DAISY. Messrs. Brown and Fitzgerald, Broadway. And my brokers are Messrs. Funk & Co., Wall Street.   You cable and ask if Daisy Mullan, of Lincoln Avenoo, is O.K. or not.

O'HAGAN. I will.   [*Jots down the names.*]   Any cable address, do you know?

DAISY. They sure have, but my memory ain't serving.

PAUL. I'd say " Fitz " would get the one, and " Funk " the other.

O'HAGAN. We didn't ask for your assistance.

PAUL. I thought you did. Pardon.

O'HAGAN. Mr. Deegan, I think at this stage we ought to cable one of those firms. . . .

DEEGAN. If you think such firms exist, by all means cable them.

DAISY. It might help you to see this here cable I got yesterday. [*Hands it to* O'HAGAN.]

O'HAGAN [*reads it.*] Mr. Deegan, this is important.

DEEGAN. What is it?

O'HAGAN. It's about house property. [*Reads.*] " Would lease or buy property on Mount Airy. Cable lowest price." [*Returns cable.*] Who is it from?

DAISY. Can't you read? It's signed Spalding.

O'HAGAN. And who is Spalding?

DAISY. He's a big real estate man. He wants to buy my whole block on Mount Airy.

PAUL. The Yankees are a go-ahead people.

O'HAGAN. Mr. Deegan, what do you think of all this?

DEEGAN. It doesn't concern me. What I want to know is: who is going to settle with the local bank?

DAISY. Why, dear, ain't the local bank got you and me both as security? I guess this slight misunderstanding won't make no difference in our affections, will it?

DEEGAN. It will make all the difference in the world. You have your property on Mount Airy, and I've mine on solid ground. There will be no alliance.

PAT. That's the style, by Moses!

MRS. DEEGAN. It takes granda.

DAISY. And how about the assignment, granda?

DEEGAN. Mr. O'Hagan will answer that.

o'hagan. Without marriage the assignment is waste paper.

daisy. But who huffs at the wedding? Not me.

o'hagan. My client has changed his mind.

paul [*with energy*]. Then, begorry, if he has he'll pay for it! Your client on his two knees promised to wed her, and if he goes back on that he must pay the piper. [*To* daisy] I'm going to see fair play, stranger. I saw him at your feet and heard you accepting him. . . .

daisy. You sure did.

paul. That's a luxury he must pay for, either in law or in equity. Go now and get your hat and vanity-bag, and we'll first settle with the bank and then consult a lawyer.

daisy. Settle with the bank, did you say?

paul. Surely. That cable in your pocket from Spalding is good for a million. And your breach of promise case is worth a round thousand.

daisy. Paul Twyning, that's my own plan in a capsule. If you back me up in this we'll make Granda Deegan and his ten-cent lawyer sit up and howl.

paul. Paul Twyning has spoken. He's at your service. Go now and get ready for the bank, and hire your cousin Darby to drive us in in state.

daisy [*animated*]. I sure will.

paul. Bring your vanity-bag and all papers.

daisy. You bet. [*Hurries out.*]

paul [*despondently*]. Well, I've been called the proudest man in Dublin; now I'm going to be the meanest clod in Ireland. I won't waste words. Daisy Mullan is a retired cook and an adventuress. [*Uproar.*]

DEEGAN. Silence! Go on, Paul. You astonish me.

PAUL. She has the six hundred pounds, safe and sound, but not another brown penny in the world.

DEEGAN [*in triumph*]. Mr. O'Hagan, was I right or wrong?

O'HAGAN. You were right. I was wrong.

DEEGAN. Paul Twyning, my friend, how did you discover this?

PAUL. I was talking to her for a quarter of an hour before you came in, and I sent her upstairs, lest she give us the slip altogether. . . .

DAN *jumps out of the cupboard.*

DAN. I'm in flames, but Paul Twyning's a just man! I was hid in there the whole time he and Daisy were talking, and heard every word they said. She told him she was a cook and her brother a janitor to a stockbroker, and she got all her property — draft and all — in the trash basket.

PAUL [*piously*]. See that, now! It always pays to speak the simple truth. . . . Who'd have thought of Dan being in the cupboard.

DEEGAN. Come forward, Daniel.

DAN. Yes, fader.

DEEGAN. Swear with uplifted hand to the truth of that statement.

DAN [*his hand up*]. Afore you and God, fader, I'm telling the truth. Amen. She said her brother give her the papers to show round here and get some ould fool with money.

O'HAGAN. That's the solution. The brother cooked everything. . . . Paul Twyning, I'm ashamed to look in your honest face. I hope you can forgive us all.

PAUL. To err is human; to forgive, divine. I freely forgive you all.

They murmur thanks and PAT *shakes hands with* PAUL.

DAN. Is that all you want with me, fader?

DEEGAN. That's all at present. For once in your life you've done me a small service.

DAN. Well, I'm going to hide in here again. . . .

DENIS *comes in, fuming.*

DENIS. Now, I want no more twistin'! My daughter's in this house, somewhere, and I mean to find her. [*To* DAN] Where's my Rose?

DAN. The Lord knows, Denis. I hain't seen her for over a week.

ROSE *comes from the cupboard, in tears and terror.*

PAUL. Now, Dan! Let the whole world see how you can defend your sweetheart. That blackthorn isn't an ornament, it's for practical purposes. Spit on the end of it and it's loaded.

DAN [*beside* ROSE *draws the stick*]. I'm in flames, but I'll defend my own Rose to the death! I'll have to fight the Black and Indians in Philadelphy, and I may as well practise a bit at home. Now, Denis, I daar you!

PAUL [*laughs*]. Emancipated! Behold Dan Deegan, emancipated!

DENIS [*going to* ROSE]. Come on, gerril. . . .

PAUL. Now, Dan Quixote, let him have it!

DAN [*with a flourish*]. Keep back! or, by all that's holy, I'll split you to the chin!

DENIS [*receding*]. I'll not lave this house without

her. And I'll give her a wiggin' when I get her home. [*Sits down.*]

DEEGAN. Paul Twyning, will you give Mr. O'Hagan and me a word in private?

PAUL. I will not. There's been far too much privacy and duplicity already. I'll answer your questions, here and now.

DEEGAN. We are not clear as to your plans.

PAUL. I can soon dispel the mist. Daisy and I are going to settle with the bank. That done, she'll want me to go with her to a lawyer, to frame up a case against Mr. Deegan. But I'll turn on my heel and say, " Begone, adventuress! Paul Twyning is not a blackmailer."

The DEEGANS *applaud.*

DENIS. Yaha! yaha!

PAUL. What are you " yahaing " about?

DENIS. At your honesty. What else?

PAUL. Instead of yaha, it's " Yahoo " you should call. For that's what you are. A Yahoo.

PAT. Ould Dublin on the Liffey! Go on, Paul.

PAUL. Now for my own terms.

DEEGAN. Oh!

PAUL. Why do you ejaculate? As a man of the world, do you expect me to cultivate wrinkles over your affairs for nothing?

DEEGAN. I expect nothing for nothing. Name your terms.

PAUL. Twenty pounds sterling. I want to take a scoot over to Chicago.

DEEGAN. I'll give you ten pounds in cash, and Daniel's ticket and portmanteau.

DAN. Flames, am I not for the water!

DEEGAN. Silence, boy. [*To* PAUL] Are you satisfied?

PAUL. Agreed.

DEEGAN. Thank you. [*To* O'HAGAN] Has Daisy Mullan a case against me for breach of contract?

O'HAGAN. She has. Once she settles with the bank she has a good case. But without Paul Twyning's evidence she has none.

PAUL. Begorry, with Dan's ocean ticket and ten pounds in my pocket, she'll have a job serving me with a summons.

The DEEGANS *applaud.*

DEEGAN. Paul Twyning, you are a man of ripe understanding. If you were in my shoes how would you meet the domestic issue?

PAUL. I'd sign the pub over to Patrick and the farm to my son Daniel, the said Patrick to pay me a small yearly rent, and the said Daniel to pay me a pound a week for life, with the use of the grey mare and trap on Sundays, market days, and Coort days.

DEEGAN. Paul Twyning, you are a gifted man. Patrick and Daniel, would that settlement shut your mouths for ever?

PAT. I'd never lip it again, father.

MRS. DEEGAN. It's more than we deserve, granda.

DEEGAN [*to* DAN]. What do you say, boy?

DAN [*lamely*]. Rose and me would be good to you, fader. You could do the plannin' and we'd do the work. Rose can milk cows and feed pigs and boil praties.

DEEGAN. That's a wise answer, boy. I'll speak to the priest and you'll be married in three days.

DENIS. She'll not come empty-handed. I'll give her thirty pound and the spotted cow.

DEEGAN. We neither want your spotted cow, nor your money, nor your friendship.

PAUL. Here, Mr. Deegan, that won't do at all. Let yourself and Denis shake hands. Dammit, life's too short to quarrel. And it's most disedifying to see two good neighbours — the backbone of the parish — at loggerheads.

DEEGAN. Denis has heard what I said. After that, if he wishes to shake hands I've no objection.

DENIS. And you heard what I said. [*Shaking hands*] I'll speak out my mind, James Deegan. I've been trying for thirty years to get a good law-shoot again you, but you always wriggled out of it, and you've tricked me again.

DEEGAN. You've had many opportunities, Denis, but you threw them away.

DENIS. Well, if I ever get a chance at Dan, I'll not throw it away. . . .

PAUL. Ah, quit talking! you rural people are the devil for law. You'd put a writ on a rabbit for trespass.

DAN. Come on, Rose, and see the new house. I'm in flames, but this is a miracle. [*He takes* ROSE *to the room.*]

PAT. Come on, Janey, we'll have a look too. [*He and* MRS. DEEGAN *go to the room.*]

PAUL. I think I hear Miss Mullan. . . .

DAISY *comes in, back, flashily dressed.*

DAISY. All here! Some more plotting, I guess.

PAUL. Mr. Deegan has just settled Dan's breach case, Miss Mullan, and I hope in due coorse he'll settle his own.

DAISY. That's up to him. I don't want no law, but I ain't no fool. If old Deegan wants a peaceable settlement, I'm ready to discuss it. . . . I've figured up your assets, Mr. Deegan, and you're worth about five thousand pounds. Don't you think one of 'em belongs to me for breach of contract?

DEEGAN. I must consult my lawyer.

DAISY. Waal, mind, I ain't coming back here with my finger in my mouth to sue for terms. If you don't want a settlement, say so, and I'll see a lawyer in town.

O'HAGAN [rising]. Mr. Deegan, I want two words with you. Come outside. [He and DEEGAN go out.]

DENIS. I'll follow them. I might hear something. [He goes out.]

DAISY. Paul Twyning, just what are you up to? You've kept me guessing right along. Just what are you up to?

PAUL. I meant to unfold my story on the way to town, but I can as well unfold myself here. I want your sweet self, Daisy.

DAISY. Whaaaaat!

PAUL. I've travelled Ireland, England, and parts of Scotland, but you're the first intelligent woman I've ever met. Now before I say another word, let me ask you a question. What do you think of my intellectual equipment?

DAISY. I think you got that roll of money.

PAUL. Emphatically right. The stuff is here. [Shows her the roll of notes.] But the bank will never thumb it. Ould Deegan can pay it off at instalments. After his long reign of local tyranny, a touch of humility will do him good. So what say you, my honey, if we spend this rowl together?

DAISY. Do you care for me, Paul?

PAUL. Amn't I sinning my sowl for you? Amn't I risking five years in gaol for you? Surely to God that answers your question. Care for you? Why, the minute I heard your voice at M'Gothigan's barn dance, I kicked off a year every time you spoke.

DAISY. And would you come to America, Paul?

PAUL. I'm getting Dan's ocean ticket and port-manteau. Two things in America I want to see. One is the Statue of Liberty, and the other is your brother that fished out the documents from the trash basket.

DAISY. But what security have I gotten that you mean a square deal by me?

PAUL. I can give good bail for my behaviour. [*Offers the roll of money.*] Put that in your bag and regulate my conduct.

DAISY. No, sweetheart, you hang on to it. I'm yours, Paul. Kiss my hand.

PAUL [*kissing her hand*]. That settles it. We'll pay Dublin a quiet visit, till this blows over, and then, as Dan says, " the raging main ".

DAISY. My cousin Darby's going to drive us in. I can pick up my suitcase at the house, passing.

PAUL. Nicely! We just have time to catch the last train, and Darby will drive home empty.

DEEGAN, O'HAGAN, *and* DENIS *come in.*

O'HAGAN. Miss Mullan, when you settle with the bank, come straight back here. I'll wait here for you. We'll have our offer prepared, and it won't be ungenerous.

DAISY. Sure. I'll come right back. Now, Paul Twyning, are you ready?

M

PAUL. Almost. I only want to see Dan . . . for the loan of his rain-coat. I can't interview bankers in these togs. [*He goes to the room.*]

DAISY. I guess you folks have gotten the soft side of Paul Twyning, I do.

DEEGAN. You are mistaken. There's no soft side to Paul Twyning.

DAISY. We'll see. I'm going now to settle with the bank. The money is here [*taps the bag*]. Not the money was stolen, but other money of my own. And mind this: I expect when I come back here to get a square deal.

DEEGAN. And you shall.

PAUL *comes in wearing* DAN'S *hat and coat and sporting the blackthorn.*

PAUL. I don't think I want the tin trunk. But, Mr. Deegan, could you oblige me in the loan of ten pounds?

DEEGAN. I think so. [*Gives him the money.*]

PAUL. Many thanks. [*Pockets it.*] Now, Miss Mullan, is your equipage ready?

DEEGAN. Darby Mullan's car is at the gate.

PAUL. Does anyone want a lift to the town?

O'HAGAN. No, thanks. We all stay here till you come back.

PAUL. Well, good-bye for the present. You won't have long to wait. [*He and* DAISY *go out.*]

DENIS. Yaha, yaha!

PAT, DAN, ROSE, *and* MRS. DEEGAN *come in.*

PAT. Are they away, father?

DENIS. They are, be God!

DEEGAN. They're off to the bank. The matter,

to all intents and purposes, is settled. Mr. O'Hagan has the agreements in the bag. Once they are signed I've no property. You have the public-house, Patrick, and Daniel has the farm. Let Daisy Mullan come back and meet an old pauper.

O'HAGAN *takes out papers and* DEEGAN *signs.*

DAN [*looking out at window*]. The car's stopped at Mullan's door, gettin' out shoot-cases.

DEEGAN. She wants to show off her American trappings in the town.

DAN. I'm in flames, but all's not right! They're away galloping down the road, and laughin' like mad.

DEEGAN. Fools like to exhibit themselves. They'll laugh less when they come back and hear my offer.

DENIS. Ay, when they come back!

DAN. I'm in flames, Paul's kissin' the ould Yankee like a steam-engine, and she's lettin' him. [*Coming from window*] Honest to God, amen, fader, all's not right! I believe you'll never see them again. . . .

DEEGAN. Never what, sir!

DAN. Oh, nothing, fader. You know best. You're a highly educated man.

DENIS. Yaha, yaha!

DAN. Paul or no Paul, Daisy or no Daisy, I've got my Rose. Amen. [*He puts his arm round her.*]

THE END

THE NEW GOSSOON

A Comedy in Three Acts

The New Gossoon was first produced in the Abbey Theatre, Dublin, on April 19, 1930, with the following cast:

ELLEN CARY, *a Farmer*	Maureen Delany
LUKE CARY, *her Son*	Denis O'Dea
PETER CARY, *an Uncle*	Michael J. Dolan
NED SHAY, *the Servant Man* . . .	P. J. Carolan
MAG KEHOE, *the Servant Girl* . . .	Frolie Mulhern
RABIT HAMIL, *a Poacher*	F. J. McCormick
SALLY HAMIL, *his Daughter*	Eileen Crowe
JOHN HENLY, *a Corn Miller* . . .	Arthur Shields
BIDDY HENLY, *his Daughter*	Shelah Richards

The action throughout takes place in Cary's kitchen
and occurs on the same night.

TIME.—The Present.

The play was produced by Arthur Shields

ACT I

A big farm-house kitchen, bright and comfortable, with evening sunshine flaming on the back windows.

The back door is open, and to right and left are other doors leading to other parts of the house.

An old motor-cycle is standing on its own rest near the back window.

MAG *comes in from the yard. She is a coarse girl, with dirty bobbed hair, about thirty-five years old.*

MAG [*flinging aside her old sun-bonnet*]. Curses on them and their hay! I wish there wasn't a hay-field in broad Ireland. [*She wipes her face and neck with a cloth.*] I'll be as red as a crab, and peeled like an onion. . . .

RABIT HAMIL *comes in, back. He looks like a full-time poacher. His hat is garnished with trout-flies, and he has two rabbit-traps and a net slung over his shoulder.*

RABIT. Where's the widow Cary?

MAG. I don't know — nor damn the hair I care! not giving you a bad answer, Rabit. . . . They've kept me working in the hay-field to within an ace of six o'clock, and now I've a day's work to do before bedtime. Cows to milk and calves to feed and pigs to feed, and potatoes to wash and boil for to-morrow morning. The man that freed the blacks in America should be President of Ireland. . . .

RABIT. Will you cease talking! If you harnessed that stream of talk you could do your work by compressed air.

MAG. Well . . . what do you want?

RABIT. Were you over in our cottage last night?

MAG. I was so. Your daughter Sally invited me
in to hear the wireless-box talking in the kitchen.

RABIT. Was Luke Cary in?

MAG. No, not in my time. Sally told me Luke
hadn't been there for weeks. Since he got this
ould motor-bike he roams the world every night.

RABIT. Are you a friend of my Sally's, or an
envoy of Cary's?

MAG. What d'ye mean by an envy of Cary's?

RABIT. I mean a spy. Did Luke Cary send you
over to pump my Sally? Maybe that's plainer.

MAG. He did not! He'd know better. And,
Rabit Hamil, you should know better too.

RABIT. The Carys have done me an injury. In
fact, they've done me two injuries. But Sally can
right her own wrong, and I'll right mine. I'm going
to raise hell's delight on this homestead.

MAG. What have they done, Rabit?

RABIT. They've put up placards on the mountain: " Trespassers prosecuted and dogs shot ".
That's what they've done — after me walking the
mountain for over thirty years.

MAG. They say your dogs worried their sheep.

RABIT. They're liars. My dogs wouldn't look at
a sheep. My dogs have more intelligence than
the Carys.

MAG. Maybe 'twas Ned Shay, the servant man,
put up the placards. Ned has a lot to say here.

RABIT. Ay, a lot to say. Where you find a widow
woman you generally find a man about the place
who's a lot to say.

MAG. Lord, Rabit, you shouldn't say them things.

[*Laughs.*] That's terrible altogether. . . . Not but she calls him " Ned, dear ", and if he gets a meal here she gives him the blue duck-egg and the big, smiling potato.

RABIT. The brains of this concern is Ned Shay, and I'm going to shift him.

MAG. Lord, Rabit, if you manage that the whole place'll fall in staves! I'd give my eyes to see it. For Ned Shay — and he only a servant here like myself — is a born slave-driver. The sweat never dries on him.

RABIT. I'll dry the sweat on him. I'll dry the sweat on more than him. If they don't take down them placards I'll destroy the breed. . . . Gimme a drink of water.

MAG. I'll give you milk, Rabit. She's a big jug of crame set up here. . . . [*She hands him the jug.*] Take a good swiggin' of it, Rabit. It's the wee Jersey cow's milk — it's thick.

RABIT. Tell me when to stop. [*Drinks.*]

MAG. Swig away at it. She'll think the cat drunk it.

RABIT. I'll lave that inch in the bottom — that the cat couldn't get at. [*Gives her jug.*] Thank you, Mag. You're a fine girl, Mag. A fine girl, according to my computing.

MAG. If you get a chance come a double back and I'll make you an egg-nog. There's fresh eggs and everything at my hand.

RABIT. You're a fine girl, Mag Kehoe. I'll come back for the egg-nog. [*Going, but turns.*] If the widow Cary hears you were in our house last night, you'll gouta this. She fired the last girl was here because she made a friend of my Sally.

MAG. I'll spend my night out where and how I like. If Mrs. Cary doesn't like that she can lump it. The day's gone by when a servant girl can be tossed about like an ould newspaper.

RABIT. If she fires you you mightn't have far to go for another post. But keep that hint to yourself. Remember: keep your lips tight on that.

MAG. Like a vice, Rabit.

RABIT. And if she fires you for sitting in my house, you could give her a wee jag about her son Luke sitting in it. Don't overdo it, you know. A hint is enough.

MAG. Lord, Rabit, you're as deep as a draw-well.

RABIT. I'll go now and interview Luke Cary in the hay-field.

MAG. He'll be here at sharp six, Rabit. He sent me in ahead to make tea. He's going somewhere on this ould rakin' machine. He's got another girl up at the corn mills, I hear.

RABIT. Sally can attend to the other girl herself. I'll confine my attack to the placards. [*He goes.*]

MAG [*busy with teapot*]. Lord, the Carys are in for a great war. . . .

ELLEN CARY *comes in, right. She is a fresh-faced woman, aged forty-four, and a worker.*

ELLEN. Mag, you've been here a year all but three days, and I never had to speak to you before. And we won't quarrel now. But your term'll be up in a few days, and maybe you'd like to make a change?

MAG. If you like. I'll make it now if you like, and shed no salt tears.

ELLEN. All right, Mag. I'll get your money. [*She is going.*]

MAG. I'll go to-morrow morning. Will that do? My shoes are away getting heeled.

ELLEN. That'll do nicely.

MAG. Aren't you going to tell me where I'm in fault? I haven't stole anything, have I?

ELLEN. I've no fault, Mag, to find with you or your work. But you're making friends of certain people that I object to.

MAG. You mean the Rabit Hamils?

ELLEN. I mentioned no names.

MAG. But you fired the last girl was here because she made a chum of Sally Hamil.

ELLEN. If I did I'd forgotten it.

MAG. I've only been in Hamil's cottage a few times — on my night out. Sally has a wireless-box in the kitchen and I wanted to hear it talking. Was there any harm in that?

ELLEN. I haven't said so.

MAG. You've more than said so, you've fired me. But you haven't objected to your son Luke listening to Sally's wireless talking.

ELLEN [*comes back*]. What's that you say, Mag?

MAG. Nothing at all.

ELLEN. When was Luke in Hamil's house?

MAG. You can ask him that. You've told me little, and I'll tell you less.

ELLEN. Mag Kehoe, you're not the girl I took you for. But no matter. You and I'll part on good terms. [*She goes out, right.*]

MAG. She can put that in her jug and jummle it!

LUKE *comes in quickly from the yard. He is a restless-looking youth, and wears flannel pants, striped shirt, and soft collar.*

LUKE. Tay, Mag, tay!

MAG. Are you in a tearing hurry?

LUKE. Ay, I'm damned apt! I've a place to go.
I ought to've started by now, and I've to shave yet.
[*He looks at motor.*]   Hurry up, Mag.

MAG [*puts down cup and saucer*]. I know where
you're going.   You're going up to the corn mills.

LUKE. Here, Kehoe! what's the matter with
you?

MAG. I'm just after being fired.

LUKE. Who fired you?

MAG. Your ma-ma.

LUKE. What for?

MAG. For sitting in Rabit Hamil's, listening to
Sally's wireless-box.

LUKE. She was right! . . . Tay!   [*Sits at table.*]

MAG. Of course you never sat listening-in? . . .

LUKE. Tay, I tell you!

RABIT *comes in.*

MAG. It's the first time ever I was dismissed on
the spot for sitting down a few minutes in a respectable neighbour's house. . . .

LUKE [*loudly*]. Tay!   Tay!

MAG *pours tea.*

RABIT. Luke Cary, I've called in about them
placards: " Trespassers prosecuted and dogs shot ".
Does that apply to me?

LUKE. It applies to everyone.   We're not going
to've our sheep worried and chased off the mountain
by a pack of mongrel dogs.

RABIT. 'Twasn't my dogs worried your sheep.

LUKE. Ned Shay seen your dogs chasing them.

RABIT. Ned Shay's a liar. And you're another if you blame my dogs.

MAG. That's the style, Rabit. Stand up to them . . . and make Sally stand up to them too.

LUKE. Mag Kehoe, if you've anything to do outside — go and do it!

MAG. I'm quit here. I needn't wet my finger again unless I like. I'm as independent now as yourselves. [*Going*] I hope the next slavey'll visit only in Captain McKane's, and not lower the dignity of the Carys. [*She goes, back.*]

LUKE. Did you come down here to call me a liar?

RABIT. I did — if necessary. And to prove it — if necessary. . . . How many sheep have you lost?

LUKE. Five. Ned Shay saw two red setters chasing them all over the mountain, and next morning we were five short.

RABIT. Will you allow me to investigate where them five sheep went?

LUKE. I'm investigating that myself. We can do our own job. We won't have to do it again. The notices are up now, and they'll stay up.

RABIT. Luke Cary, I don't particularly want to fight. I want to give you a chance to back out dacently. Your father, that's dead and in his grave, gave me liberty to trap and snare and shoot the whole mountain. And from that day to this nobody has objected.

LUKE. Well, it's time somebody objected. I'm coming into this property in a few more days, and I'll stand no nonsense. I can rent the shooting of the mountain to Captain McKane for ten pounds a year, but he doesn't want a professional poacher thrown in.

RABIT. So it's to be war?

LUKE. Call it war if you like. The notices are up to stay.

RABIT. Well, we know now where we are. You say the placards are up to stay, and I say I'll make you take them down. You clearly understand that now?

LUKE. I understand. Go ahead. [*He sees* NED *passing window and shouts*] Hi, Ned Shay! come in here a minute.

NED *comes in. A good type of intelligent farm-hand, turned forty years of age. He has a hay-rake in his hand.*

RABIT. Ned, I'm awful sorry to hear that my dogs chased five sheep off the mountain.

LUKE. Don't answer him, Ned.

NED. Was it your dogs, Rabit?

RABIT. Didn't you see my two setters chasing after them?

NED. No, I did not. Who says I did?

RABIT. Ask Luke. He'll tell you. [*Goes out, back.*]

LUKE. What the blazes did you say that for?

NED. What else could I say? I never seen Hamil's dogs chasing the sheep. His dogs are too well trained for that.

LUKE. I seen them myself, then!

NED. If you did, that's all right. But I didn't. And I want no truck with Rabit Hamil. I don't like that artificial smile he has on his face — like a weasel.

LUKE. Do you want me to go and take the notices down?

NED. I wish you hadn't put them up. But maybe you know best. If you can afford to quarrel with Rabit Hamil, let them stay up. Otherwise, I'd advise you to take them down.

LUKE. I disregard Rabit Hamil — and the breed of him! Where's my mother?

NED. She and Mag are in the byre. I don't know what's happened, but Mag's quitting us. And she was a fine worker.

LUKE. And a fine talker!

NED. That follows. They all talk, but Mag can work too.

LUKE. Aren't you going home now?

NED. Very shortly. My God, man, it's barely six o'clock. I hate to quit the place so early, and so much to be done.

LUKE. It's after six — a few minutes. Why can't you bundle up and go home at six o'clock? And not hang around here looking for something to do. You'd no call to come across here at all, you could have gone home from the hay-field.

NED. Well, I'll know what to do again.

LUKE. I want to cut out the fifteen-hour day on the farm, and I want you to help me.

NED. Surely. I'll do anything you say. But you know how it is. I've always worked here late and early, and I can't drop an old habit all of a sudden.

LUKE. I want to stop myself at six o'clock, and I can't go away and leave you working — can I?

NED. No, 'twould look bad. I understand, Luke. But you see, it's your mother still pays me on Saturday night.

LUKE. 'Tis I'll soon be paying you myself.

NED. Surely. I know that too. Then I'll start

and stop work at any minute you like.

LUKE. Well, slide away home now, or she'll come along and find you a job. . . .

ELLEN *comes in.*

ELLEN. Ned, dear, them pigs haven't a straw to lie on, and their house is in a puddle. I think they've torn a plank off the floor. Could you look in at them.

NED. Surely. I'll attend to them. [*He is going.*]

LUKE. Ned, you'd better take down them notices. . . . Maybe 'twasn't Hamil's dogs worried the sheep after all.

NED. Right, Luke. I'll attend to that.

ELLEN. See to the pigs first, Ned.

NED. I will surely. [*He goes.*]

ELLEN. Luke, will you not eat so quickly! What's the use of taking stomach drops if you eat like that?

LUKE. I'm in a hurry. I've a place to go.

ELLEN. You didn't get the hay finished.

LUKE. A couple of hours'll finish it in the morning.

ELLEN. But, sure, a couple of hours'd finish it to-night. And look at that glorious weather God has sent for it.

LUKE. Ned Shay's going home, and I can't finish it alone.

ELLEN. Ned Shay's not far away — if you want him. Ned's been here for twenty years and never wanted to stop at six o'clock before.

LUKE. Ned and I've arranged to stop work at six o'clock, like other people. And we're going to do it. [*Rising*] I'm not going to work in the fields to dark night, and then crawl into bed! [*He stumps off, right.*]

ELLEN [*to the motor*]. Oh, bad luck to you, and to

the man that invented you! Broken necks and broken hearts and broken homes! [*Picks up a hammer.*] I don't know where to hit you! If I knew where the mainspring is I'd smash it to fragments. . . .

RABIT *comes in.*

RABIT. Are you doing a bit of motor mechanic-ing, Ellen? Or maybe you're going to give the mechanic a job?

ELLEN. I'm not touching it, Rabit. Not but I hate the sight of it and the rattle of it and smell of it.

RABIT. And the danger of it!

ELLEN. Ah, quit talking. Isn't that why Luke got it for a few pounds? The last owner of it was launched into Eternity.

RABIT. A few pounds? Is that all you know? Luke paid a bright penny for it.

ELLEN. Six pounds he told me, and he'd the money of his own — the proceeds of a greyhound pup

RABIT. Twenty pounds, Ellen, he paid for it and the harness. But don't make me anything the worse.

ELLEN. What harness?

RABIT. The leather coat, the helmet, and the goggles. Twenty pounds for all.

ELLEN. But where'd Luke get twenty pounds — these times?

RABIT. I can tell you that too. He won eight pounds on a dog they call Owen Roe O'Nail, and lost two of it the same night on a bitch they call Red Maeve. That left him six in pocket. Then he sold five of your sheep off the mountain for ten pounds, and borrowed the remainder from a certain party. . . . And there's where he banked it [*the*

N

motor]. A skilled man tells me it isn't worth thirty shillings.

ELLEN. Sold five of my sheep! Lord, is that where the sheep went!

RABIT. That's where the sheep went, Ellen. He blamed my dogs for chasing them off the mountain, and put up placards to give colour to it. But I knew all the time where the sheep went. I was on the mountain at daybreak, laying snares, when the butcher's boy come and took them away. The five sheep on the rumps were marked with red daubs, the way he'd made no mistake.

ELLEN. Rabit Hamil, this is terrible. Luke's going to ruin himself, and me too. . . . But you're not going to be shut off the mountain. My husband — God rest him! — gave you liberty to come and go, and while I'm here your privilege'll stay with you.

RABIT. God bless you, Ellen. I'd expect nothing else from you but the height of kindness. But I suppose Luke's come of age now, and new kings make new laws.

ELLEN. Luke isn't twenty-one till next Tuesday.

RABIT. And then he comes into farm and all?

ELLEN. Oh, I wouldn't say that, Rabit. I think I'll have my day here.   I think I deserve it.

RABIT. And a nice, quiet day you'll have. He's racing to the town every night on this devil's needle of a thing, and if he doesn't break his own neck he'll kill somebody else. And if he doesn't do that he'll come home some night with a town hussy perched on that tail-board at the back. [*Points*] That's what that bracket behind is for — for a town hussy to sit on, with her brazen face and her bare legs shaming the world.

ELLEN. True, Rabit.   Too true.

RABIT. Ay, and sometimes she hanging on to him at the back, with her arms fastened round his middle — and they going at fifty mile an hour.

ELLEN. It's terrible altogether.   What's to be done with him, Rabit?   You know everything — how he's behaving himself — and I know nothing.   Nobody tells me anything.

RABIT. There's only one cure for him, Ellen. Pick out a good country girl, one with a right smart edge on her, and tie him to her.   She'd soon put the notion of this whirligig out of his head.

ELLEN. I wish 'twas done.   But he says he'll never marry a country girl.

RABIT. And will you let him bring a town hussy in here?   To put the price of all you grow in high-heel shoes and silk stockings and jumpers?   Mind, Ellen, that's what's brewing.   This implement [*the motor*] 'll get him into trouble — if he's not in it already. . . . But don't make me anything the worse.

ELLEN. I'll make you nothing the worse, Rabit. Every word you say is true.   Nothing but trouble can come of this roaming wild at night.

RABIT. I know five farmers' sons who've come to grief already, and every one of them had an implement like this [*the motor*].   Three of them broke their necks instantaneously, and the other two had to marry town hussies — at the last minute.

ELLEN. I know the two you mean.

RABIT. And you know what use they are in a farm-house!   They couldn't throw a pick to a hen.

ELLEN. True.   They're only for driving a man to the door.

RABIT. Now, Ellen, as the talk has come round, that Sally girl of mine — if your son'd the grace to see it — would make him a targin-fine wife.

ELLEN. Oh, Sally's a right wee girl.

RABIT. I declare to heaven, Ellen Cary, she's a living miracle in the house. When were you in our house?

ELLEN. The time your wife died — I suppose that's a dozen years ago.

RABIT. Ah, you wouldn't know us now at all. Sally's turned the place into a bandbox. Wireless talking in the kitchen, and a sewing-machine in the corner, and the walls done with blue whitewash. . . . She went a winter to the Teck-school and it fair put the lady on her. She can make nine kinds of soup out of a rabbit.

ELLEN. Oh, Sally's a bright girl.

RABIT. You must call and see the house, Ellen. It'll take the breath from you. Painted and papered and blinds on the windows, and a geranium in full bloom in a pot — you'd think you were walking into Captain McKane's, of Checker Hall.

ELLEN. Oh, Sally has good hands.

RABIT. Hands! Look at these socks — she knit them. Look at this shirt — she made it. Look at this waistcoat — she faced it. Look at the flies in my hat — she tied them. She could make a pound a week at flies alone. I declare to heaven, Ellen Cary, she's a new wonder, a new blessing in the house, every hour of the day . . . and singing away at her work.

MAG *comes in.*

MAG. Ned Shay wants the mistress.

ELLEN. Where is he?

MAG. He's inside with the pigs. They've torn up the floor and ate the planks.

ELLEN. I knew they were in some mischief. [*She goes out.*]

MAG. Lord, Rabit, Ned Shay's in a terrific state of mind! He wanted to see you. Luke told him to take down the placards.

RABIT. Well, they've missed the last bus. I've given herself a chapter of Luke, and Sally'll give her the rest of it.

MAG. Is Sally coming here?

RABIT. She's on her way. I've won my heat, and Sally can attend to her own. If she doesn't make this clown marry her, she can make him pay up. Hard money's as good as matrimony.

MAG. And I go hence in the morning.

RABIT. You're not going far hence. If I get Sally off my hands, you're coming over to me.

MAG. To you! What to do, Rabit?

RABIT. To spend your days with me, and look after me, and take care of me. For I haven't got a dacent meal since my wife died. Look at me — like an ould-age pensioner, and I not turned fifty! I tell you, Mag Kehoe, I'm starved and badgered and neglected. Damn-all Sally can do but look in the glass and powder her snout. If ever she gets a man he'll have to live on the wireless.

MAG. Lord, Rabit, I never thought of this outcome! I never thought you'd behold me in that way. Mind, Rabit, I'd make you a snug wife. And you'd be kind to me, wouldn't you?

RABIT. I'm kind to all that's kind to me. But cross me and I'd fight like a badger in a trap.

MAG. Lord, Rabit, I'd do every mortal thing for you. I'd study your needs morning, noon, and night. . . . My heart! if Sally knew of this. . . .

RABIT. Sally and I are finished. If she doesn't marry this pet madman, she'll get a bit of money and go to Scotland — to the married sister.

MAG. And when'd you and I make the great change in our condition, Rabit?

RABIT. The minute Sally walks out, you walk in. But keep all this to yourself. No talk, remember, or you'll snap the trap empty.

MAG. I never thought I'd be a married lady! I'd stopped thinking about it altogether. . . . We'll be quick about doing it, Rabit. I've a good bit of money in the Post Office. ... . I'll be married in a red dress with blue borders——

ELLEN *comes in*.

ELLEN. Mag, where's the hatchet?

MAG. I know where it is — I was chopping sticks with it.

ELLEN. Ned Shay wants it.

MAG. I'll go and get him it. [*She goes.*] ·

ELLEN. Rabit, you must excuse me. I'm going to the milk-house.

RABIT. Surely. But isn't that my errand here — milk. Our cow's bone dry, and we haven't white milk in the house. Could you spare us a pint in the day?

ELLEN. We've plenty of milk. Have you a jug?

RABIT. Sally'll come for the milk, and be glad to get it. . . . And isn't this Kehoe girl quitting here?

ELLEN. She's leaving to-morrow morning.

RABIT. You're doing the wise thing, Ellen, to

get rid of her — she talks too much. . . . But don't make me anything the worse.

ELLEN. I won't mention your name, Rabit.

RABIT. Till you get another girl, make my Sally give you a hand to bake and wash and milk——

SALLY comes in, with a jug in her hand. She is twenty years old, and wears a bright jumper and coloured skirt. Her hair is newly waved, and she is smoking a cigarette.

SALLY. Well, Rabit: are you here?

RABIT. I was in bespeaking the milk. You'll get a pint in the day and welcome. . . . Put that cigar out of your mouth!

SALLY. Can you spare it, Mrs. Cary?

ELLEN. Surely, Sally, we've oceans of milk.

RABIT. Mag Kehoe's quitting here to-morrow, and you'll give Ellen a hand to bake and milk and wash up. . . .

SALLY. Oh, is this Luke's motor-bike? [*She sets her hip on the carrier.*]

RABIT. Come away outa that! Don't be parchin' yourself up on that tailboord like a town hussy.

SALLY. I'd love to go tearing down the road on it — a thousand mile an hour!

RABIT. Come off it, I say!

SALLY. The last picture I was at — he carried her off in an aeroplane.

RABIT. He'd soon pitch her out, and let her walk home. . . . Come off the tailboord, I say!

SALLY. I'd love to be able to stunt with it. [*She touches the horn.*]

RABIT [*leaps*]. Will you stop it, I tell you! If it starts buzzin' 'twill tear down the house.

ELLEN. Luke's in the room, Sally.

SALLY. Well, I'm doing no harm.

RABIT. Come off the tailboord altogether!

LUKE *comes in. He is in full harness: overalls, leather coat, helmet, and gauntlets stuck in his belt. He also has a watch on his wrist, and a cigarette hung on his lip.*

LUKE [*angrily*]. Who's touching my machine?

SALLY. 'Twas me, Luke. I only touched the horn.

LUKE. Well, leave it alone! What do you know about a machine?

SALLY. Good Lord, it doesn't need a mechanical genius to blow the horn!

LUKE. You leave it be, then! If the horn wants blowing I'll attend to it myself.

RABIT. Come off the tailboord altogether!

SALLY [*coming off*]. One'd think you'd invented this old crock yourself — out of scraps.

LUKE. Don't you tamper with it again. Keep away from it altogether. That's all.

He glances importantly at his watch and goes back to the room.

ELLEN. Luke's in a bad temper, Sally. . . . Give me your jug, I'll go and get the milk. [*She takes jug and goes.*]

RABIT. What the divil took you up on that tailboord, like a town hussy, and she watching you!

SALLY. Why, what harm was in it?

RABIT. Every harm in it. She'd like you better if you'd taken your two feet and kicked the engine out of it.

SALLY. What do I care whether she likes me or

not? I'm not going to lick after Ellen Cary. If I get anything here I'll have to fight for it. . . . Go you outside. I want to speak to Luke.

RABIT. It's the mother you must speak to first, I tell you!

SALLY. That used to be the idea, but we do our own job now. Go on, fade out. I know what I'm doing.

RABIT. Luke comes into the farm next Tuesday. If you don't nail him now you'll never nail him.

SALLY. Go on, and keep the mother outside. I've got him nailed already.

RABIT. That's the style. . . . I didn't know you'd the hook in him. I'll keep Ellen outside till you're ready.

SALLY. If I touch the horn — you and Ellen both rush in on us.

RABIT. My sowl, you're not slow. You haven't attended the pictures for nothing.

SALLY. I'm touching it now for Luke. [*She blows it.*] Go on, get!

RABIT. I'm away. [*He goes.*]

LUKE *comes in.*

SALLY. It's me again, Luke. Are you angry?

LUKE. I am! What brought you down here at all? What are you and Rabit after?

SALLY. I'm down for a pint of milk, and Rabit was in bespeaking it. Is there any harm in that?

LUKE. Ah, I'm not so green. The pint of milk's only an excuse. Rabit's setting some of his traps round here, but he won't trap me.

SALLY. My father's got nothing to do with this

at all. I can look after myself. You and I started this line on our own, and we can dispose of it our-selves.

LUKE. D'ye want my mother to know—is that your game?

SALLY. I'm not a bit particular who knows. And you needn't try to bounce me, Luke.—Standing there, all dolled up like Kaye Don.

LUKE. Will you meet me down the road in half an hour? Down at the bridge?

SALLY. You want to let me see how much dust you can make? Isn't that the idea?

LUKE. No, I'll stop. Honest.

SALLY. You mightn't get this old crock started again. We can settle it here.

LUKE. There, I want no more talk! I've a place to go. [*He tries to move the machine.*]

SALLY [*stops him*]. You're not going yet. I want a few words with you.

LUKE. Let go the machine!

SALLY. I'll box your ears for you! You're not going to fool or frighten me — mind that! I want to know what you're up to? You haven't seen me for three weeks.

LUKE. Will you not talk so loud. You'll have her in on me.

SALLY. No fear. I told Rabit to keep her outside till I'm through with you.

LUKE. I thought so! I knew there was a trap in it. . . . You and your pint of milk!

SALLY. Here, let's cut out the frills. You promised to marry me when you came into the farm. You come into it next Tuesday. Are you ready to marry me on Wednesday? I'm ready now.

LUKE. But I'm not.

SALLY. Well, you can have a little time. I'm not in that big a rush. . . . When'll you be ready?

LUKE. Sally, I wish you'd meet me down at the bridge, we can't talk here.

SALLY. We can talk here, all right. Sure, 'twill only take you a minute to name the day. This is June. Will it be in July, or August, or September?

LUKE. Give me a while to think it over.

SALLY. I'll give you one red minute.

LUKE. One minute? And then what?

SALLY. I'll show you what.

LUKE [angrily]. Here, look you — to blazes outa this! I'm not going to stand here talking all night to you — Rabit Hamil's daughter!

SALLY [slaps him]. What's the matter with Rabit Hamil's daughter! She was a bit too slick for you — that's all her faults.

LUKE [tugging]. Let go the machine! Let go the machine——

SALLY [hangs on to it]. You won't leave this house till you've heard me out. Then you can mount your old potato-digger, and tear off — to blazes if you like!

LUKE. I'll run the machine over you!

SALLY. Not without blowing the horn! [She blows horn loudly.] Now, young man: you've spilled the beans.

RABIT in the doorway.

RABIT. What's this, this, this! Hi, murdher, Ellen Cary!

ELLEN comes in.

ELLEN. For heaven's sake! what's all the noise? What's wrong?

LUKE. Nothing at all! [*He makes a bolt for the room.*]

SALLY [*grabs the belt*]. Not so fast! You'll stay here and face the music — or I'll scratch your eyes out of the sockets!

ELLEN. Sally, what's he done?

SALLY. He promised to marry me, Mrs. Cary, and now he's trying to hedge.

LUKE. It's a lie! I never promised to marry her. I never made a contract of the kind.

SALLY. You never made a contract? Were you ever making anything but contracts? Weren't you running after me like a nightmare? If I went for a pail of water, you were sitting at the well moaning.

LUKE. 'Twasn't for you I was moaning!

SALLY. No, you were moaning for somebody else. For your dead granny.

LUKE. I wasn't near the well. Or if I was — 'twas getting water for our own cattle.

RABIT. Now, Luke: I seen you there myself, and heard you moaning. For whole days you sat there — and your mother thought you were hoeing in the field.

SALLY. If I went out to milk the cow, you were sitting under a bush — hunched up like a hedgehog. Is that a lie?

LUKE. It is a lie!

RABIT. Now, Luke: I've seen you there myself innumerable times — sitting in a heap. I often thought you were dead.

SALLY. If I went out with the calf's drink, you were waiting for me — more of a calf than the one

I was going to feed. And, sure, we couldn't go to bed for you at night — sitting plastered up against the hob like a lump of dough.

RABIT. Ay, or bird-lime.

ELLEN. Was he in your house, Rabit?

RABIT. Was he what? He sat a whole year in it — glued to the chair.

LUKE. I don't bother you much now.

RABIT. And you couldn't believe what a relief it is. . . . Of course, Sally misses you. But I never was in love with you.

SALLY. And I'm not going to suffer that long, boring purgatory for nothing. I wouldn't break in another greenhorn for a thousand pounds.

ELLEN. Did he promise to marry you, Sally? That's the question.

SALLY. He asked me at least a thousand times, Mrs. Cary. At every hour of the day and night, and in every nook and corner within a round mile of the house. And always the same plaint — " Sally, will you marry me? " Till at last, to get the ding of it out of my ears, I said I would.

ELLEN. Did he give you a ring?

LUKE. No fear! I wasn't so green.

SALLY. Oh, no; you're a very clever fellow. A Don Juan you are, or think you are. But I'll tell you before your own mother what you are: you're the biggest galoot in the parish. If a girl throws an eye at you, you run after her till she has to throw a brick at you.

LUKE. It's a lie. It's them runs after me. I can't get walking the road for them.

SALLY. Ah, help! listen to that. . . . Why, you dough-head! the little schoolgirls go into giggles at you racing up and down the road on that old bucket-shop, and you rigged out like an Atlantic flier. The very cows pause and look after you.

ELLEN. Luke, did you promise to marry this girl?

LUKE. No, I did not.

ELLEN. Did you give her any presents?

LUKE. Not likely!

SALLY. Because you never had one penny to rattle with another. Sure the day of the trip you couldn't buy a banana.

LUKE. Nor for you, anyhow.

ELLEN. Did you write any letters, Luke?

SALLY. He did, and delivered them himself. He was his own postmaster-general.

ELLEN. Luke, did you put pen to paper?

LUKE. If I did she burnt them.

SALLY. Did she indeed!

LUKE. You said you did. I burnt yours.

SALLY. Oh, I hadn't the heart to burn yours. I've got hundreds of them, and they'll be rare stuff for the newspapers. I never read them myself — they were that long and stupid. . . . And now you're writing the same slop all over again to Biddy Henly, of the corn mills.

LUKE [*shouting*]. If you say that again I'll kick you and Rabit down the road!

RABIT [*drawing a trap*]. Say it again, Sally — till we see what foot he kicks with.

ELLEN. Rabit Hamil, have some sense . . . and some pity for me.

RABIT. I will, Ellen. For the moment I forgot the mother. . . . Come on home, Sally. You've a case without a flaw in it, and you're the girl can handle it.

ELLEN. Sally, you'll let me see one letter in Luke's writing: then I'll know who to believe.

SALLY. Certainly, Mrs. Cary. I'll bring down the whole bagful to-morrow. And what's more: I'll let you put your hand in, like into a lottery bag, and draw out one letter: and if it doesn't contain a promise of marriage, I'll burn the whole collection and never mention Luke's name again.

ELLEN. That's very fair, Sally. But could you not let me see a letter to-night? His Uncle Peter's coming, and I want to lay all this before him.

SALLY. Right, Mrs. Cary. I'll come back and bring a fistful of them——

LUKE [shouts]. Roast the whole breed of ye — Rabit Hamils! Rabit Hamils! [He tears off to the room.]

RABIT. Ellen, your son doesn't behave like an innocent man.

ELLEN. I never knew he did more than bid the time of day to Sally. I never knew he set foot in your house.

SALLY. Of course you didn't. Your far fields are beside our cottage, and Luke could be over the fence a million times a day without you knowing it. But honest, Mrs. Cary, he was a fair plague to us. I was the first girl he ever fell for, and 'twas such a discovery that he went clean crazy. He'd sit all day long — like a sheep-dog — watching me at my work, leaving me only to go home for his meals and then come straight back to me. . . . And now he's after Biddy Henly, of the corn mills, and I'm not going to let him off with it.

RABIT. Right, Sally. You'll get a hundred pounds for your broken heart, and you can go to Scotland.

ELLEN. Ah now, Rabit, be easy. Sally's heart isn't broken beyond repair — is it, Sally?

SALLY. There isn't a chip off it, nor a crack in it.

RABIT. Careful, Sally! Mind what you're saying. I know you're a smart girl. But that's dangerous talk and you going to law. [*To* ELLEN] She's trying to hide the feelings, Ellen, as any young girl'd do. But, sure, I hear her every night pacing the room — sobbing and lamenting.

ELLEN. Do you walk the room like that, Sally?

SALLY. If I do it must be in my sleep. The love business isn't the same now, Mrs. Cary, as when you were in it. A man could sneak after a girl for twenty years, and then sneak off with himself; and she, poor thing, would be too proud to mention it. But now a young girl uses her head first and her heart after, and she doesn't care a damn who knows it.

ELLEN. I know, Sally, it's like that in big cities, but I didn't think the change had come this far.

SALLY. A change for the better soon travels into far places. I've built myself a three-valve set and can listen-in to London or Paris while I'm drying the dishes.

RABIT. She can, Ellen. Honest to God, she can hear a Frenchman scoulding his wife in Paris. She has it tied to a tree.

ELLEN. It's a great change has come to us. I hope it's for the better.

SALLY. Of course it's for the better. The more one knows the better. The man doesn't come now and buy a girl like a sheep. And he has to watch his step or pay the piper. The country has fewer prigs of men to-day than ever it had.

RABIT. She's well up, Ellen.

ELLEN. But, Sally, you wouldn't want Luke to marry you if he didn't like you.

SALLY. If he didn't like me he shouldn't have asked me. I wasn't chasing after him. He liked me well enough till he got this old lawn-mower. And I liked him well enough till he turned out a rotter. And what's more, Mrs. Cary, you may thank me for keeping him straight the last year. If he'd met as big a fool as himself there'd be more trouble in Ireland long ago.

ELLEN. All this sounds strange to my old-fashioned ears.

RABIT. Doesn't it now? My own ears can barely take it in at all. Often I ask myself to what race of people does Sally belong? But she's a good wee girl, Ellen. I'll say that for her.

SALLY. I'm no better than other wee girls, and don't pretend to be. If Luke Cary'd played the game I wouldn't give him away for a million. But he's a rotter, and I'll make him sit up. . . . Mrs. Cary, how much is the milk?

ELLEN. Nothing, Sally. And I'll give you a jug of milk night and morning if you come for it.

SALLY. Thanks, Mrs. Cary. I'll come for it.

ELLEN. And don't forget the letter, Sally.

SALLY. No fear, Mrs. Cary. [*She goes.*]

RABIT. Could you believe it, Ellen? Could you believe that Sally's my wee girl, still in her 'teens, and raired at the back of a mountain?

ELLEN. Whether I believe it or not, it's true. Sally's a new symptom. And so is Luke.

RABIT. She'd make a man of him, Ellen. She's as straight herself as a new nail, and she'd make

O

him toe the line or she'd knock his brains out. . . .
She'd turn on myself in a minute.

SALLY *comes in and lays her jug on the table.*

SALLY. I forgot to throw this old potato-digger
out of joint. He won't see Biddy Henly on it
to-night.

*She gets a spanner, kneels down, and takes out the
plug.*

You keep that plug, Mrs. Cary, till it suits you to
give it up. 'Twill take Luke about a week to locate
what's wrong, for he barely knows enough to blow
the horn.

ELLEN. Thanks, Sally. [*Puts the plug in her pocket.*]
His Uncle Peter's coming to-night, and I didn't
want Luke going out.

SALLY. Any time you want to upset his programme,
take off the tension-wire and screw out the plug.
And any time you want to destroy it finally, take it
out to the yard and put a match to the tank; then
stand back and let it rip. If I were in your shoes
I'd burn it to a crisp.

She takes the jug and goes.

ELLEN. For all her big talk she's jealous of the
other girl.

RABIT. She is, of coorse! That's one thing they
can't shorten or shingle — jealousy. Thank God,
there's still something left to torture them!

LUKE *comes in.*

LUKE. Are you still here! Are you going to
stand there gassing all night?

RABIT. I'm going now.

LUKE. It's about time. Shift yourself, and don't come back. If you want law, go ahead.

ELLEN. Rabit Hamil, you're welcome to stay here as long as you like, and come back when you please. And you'll walk the mountain as usual. I'm still mistress here.

RABIT. And long may you reign!

ELLEN. I'd like you to see his Uncle Peter if you could manage it.

RABIT. Why, surely: Peter Cary and I are old friends. I'll be here, Ellen. And so'll Sally. Certainly, surely! [*He goes.*]

ELLEN. Isn't this a nice mess you've got yourself into with them vermin?

LUKE [*putting on gauntlets*]. I'm in no mess at all. What do I care about the Hamils! Not a spittle.

ELLEN. You'll care more before they've done with you. You're in the trap now, and they won't let you out easy.

LUKE. I'm in no trap at all. I was only in their house a few times — listening to the wireless. That's all lies about me sitting a year in it, and writing hundreds of letters. I never put pen to paper.

ELLEN. Would Sally Hamil offer to bring a bagful of letters here if they weren't in existence?

LUKE. If they bring any letters here, they've written them. I wrote no letters.

ELLEN. Didn't you tell Sally in my own hearing that you'd burnt her letters, and she'd promised to burn yours? What did you mean by that?

LUKE. 'Twas a few post cards I sent her. I didn't want her showing them all round the country.

ELLEN. Is there not a word of truth in Sally's story?

LUKE. Not a word.

ELLEN. Nor a word of lie in yours?

LUKE. Not a word.

ELLEN. Tell me this. How much did you pay for that accursed motor?

LUKE. Six pounds.

ELLEN. And what did you sell my five sheep for? — and say they were chased off the mountain.

LUKE. Who — who says that?

ELLEN. Never mind who says it. I'm asking you a simple question. What did you sell my sheep for?

LUKE. Can't I sell a few sheep if I want to? Don't I come into the farm next Tuesday — stock and all?

ELLEN. Don't be too sure. You may only come into the farm at my death — if I care to leave it that way.

LUKE. Is that the next of it!

ELLEN. Yes, that's the next of it.

LUKE. Well, I'll believe it when I see my father's will. You've kept it hidden from me long enough.

ELLEN. You'll see your father's will when it suits me — not a moment sooner.

LUKE. I'll see it next Tuesday — or I'll know for why. You've treated me like an infant long enough.

ELLEN. I won't treat you like an infant any more. And you won't treat me like a fool. You'll put those five sheep back on the mountain, or lay the price of them in my hand, or I'll see Captain McKane — this very night — and lay you in gaol.

LUKE [laughs]. I'm greatly afraid of your threats. I've heard them all before.

ELLEN. You won't hear them again. I'll take a

leaf out of Sally Hamil's book and protect myself from rascals like you.

LUKE. Rascals!

ELLEN. ~~Yes,~~ rascals. Sally calls you a rotter. But I call you ~~by the old Irish name~~ — a rascal! Something queer has swept through my mind in the last few minutes — like an explosion of old beliefs. I see myself, the old-fashioned fool mother, expecting nothing from you but a snap if anything displeased you, and content with myself if you didn't bite too deep.

LUKE. What are you talking about?

ELLEN. It's no wonder you ask. I hardly know myself what I'm saying. I'm talking, maybe, like an old slave on the edge of freedom. I've toiled for you with my own two hands — held the plough myself like a man, with you tied in a shawl at the end of the field. I could have married again and had a good man to work for me, or with me, but I never gave it a thought. 'Twas enough to've a good home for you when you grew up. And see what I've got: a lazy, selfish, headstrong rascal, and about half wise. That's what I'm talking about.

LUKE [*looks at watch*]. I haven't time to hear any more now, but I'll listen to you broadcasting another time. You'll be on again soon — you're that good at it.

ELLEN. Your Uncle Peter — your father's brother — is coming to-night, and I'll lay everything before him.

LUKE. What's all this sudden commotion about? Is it because the time has come to let me into my own? Uncle Peter hasn't bothered us much lately.

ELLEN. I sent him word to come down here to-night, and I'm glad now I did. He should be here shortly. Why not wait and hear what we have to say? He'd love to see you in that kit.

LUKE. Tell him if he wants to see me he can wait till I come back. [*He is wheeling out.*]

ELLEN. Will you be late?

LUKE. I don't know. Leave the key on the window-sill.

ELLEN. Never again! I'll lock my door at bed-time. If you're not in you can wait outside till I come and open it.

LUKE. You'll leave the key on the window-sill!

ELLEN. Well, if it isn't there you'll know I forgot. Go on, now, and don't waste your precious time.

LUKE. Don't forget to tell Uncle Peter I'm a rascal. Tell him you can't get me to say my prayers at your knee and go to bed at seven o'clock, New Time. [*He wheels out.*]

ELLEN. You won't go far to-night, anyhow; thanks to Sally Hamil. [*She takes the plug from her pocket and lays it on the dresser.*]

Curtain

ACT II

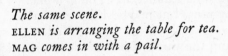

The same scene.
ELLEN *is arranging the table for tea.*
MAG *comes in with a pail.*

ELLEN. Mag, where did the jug of cream go?

MAG. I seen Luke drinking it.

ELLEN. Luke doesn't often drink sweet milk.

MAG. He came in boiling hot from the hay-field, and flew at it.

ELLEN. Well. . . . Maybe you'd like to go now for your shoes?

MAG. I'll go after a bit. [*She has put hot water in the pail and is going out.*]

ELLEN. Tell Ned Shay before he goes home I want to see him.

MAG. Here he is.

As MAG *goes out* NED *comes in.*

ELLEN. Uncle Peter's coming, Ned. You'll stay and have a cup of tea with him. I want you and him to've a talk about Luke.

NED. Has Luke gone?

ELLEN. He hasn't gone far. He's running up and down the road. Sally took a spring out of the machine and he won't be able to start it.

NED. My God, you shouldn't have let Sally do that! 'Twill only madden him, and he's mad enough.

ELLEN. 'Twill keep him within easy reach of the house. I want the uncle to see him and talk to him.

209

I'm going to tell Peter every mortal thing, and let him advise me for the best. I couldn't put up with this at all.

NED. Well, I told Luke I was going home. I'd better slip away now, but maybe I'll come back.

ELLEN. It's very early to go home, Ned, and so much to do about the yard. I haven't seen the place as dirty and ragged in twenty years.

NED. It isn't easy for me to know what to do. I'm between two fires. Luke wants me to stop at six, and you want me to work all night.

ELLEN. Is it Luke or I pays you?

NED. It's you. I told him so.

ELLEN. Then let Luke mind his own business. 'Twill be time enough for him to issue orders when he gets the reins. For the present I hold them.

NED. All right. I'll have no tea. But I'll go out and square up the yard. [*Pausing at the door.*] And, if Luke comes back and finds me working time he won't like it.

ELLEN. If he says anything send him to me!

NED. If he says anything I'll probably send him to hell.

ELLEN. Ned, you mustn't quarrel with Luke — just at this time.

NED. Isn't that what I'm trying to avoid — a quarrel? But you don't seem to notice it. . . . You surely don't think I'd take any cheek from your cub of a son?

ELLEN. You're right, Ned. I didn't see it that way. You've no need to take cheek from anyone. . . . I see you're as worried as myself.

NED. I'm sick of it. A man's work is nothing to it. I'm disgusted with the whole thing. . . .

For twenty years I've been my own boss here.

ELLEN. And a hard master you'd to serve. You didn't spare yourself.

NED. You don't know it. I've worked like a horse. The longest day in summer was always too short for me.

ELLEN. You've left your mark on the farm.

NED. I'm glad of it. I don't care now who comes after me. They can't take more out of it, because they can't put more into it.

ELLEN. We both took a foolish pride in hard work.

NED. There's no blessing in God's world like hard work and a quiet mind. The time I was interned — doing nothing all day long nearly killed me.

ELLEN. All our work here may go for nothing.

NED. Good honest digging never goes for nothing. Work is its own reward.

ELLEN. What's to become of Luke?

NED. I wish I knew that. I lose a lot of sleep trying to solve that problem. But it beats me. Luke's a hard thing to analyse. Sometimes I'd be talking to him and he wouldn't hear a word of it — the mind wandering away on something else. At other times he's as good a worker, and as keen a worker, and as kindly a young fellow as in Ireland.

ELLEN. Did you know he paid twenty pounds for that accursed motor?

NED. I knew the party he got it from, and knew he wouldn't get it too cheap. Luke at this stage is what you call a sucker.

ELLEN. Did you know he sold the five lost sheep?

NED. I'd an idea they didn't fly away. But they

were gone before I knew, and making a row wouldn't bring them back.

ELLEN. Did you know he was gambling on greyhounds?

NED. For heaven's sake, ask me no more! I know Luke's a spoiled boy, and that covers everything.

ELLEN. You know, Ned, you ought to've told me he was frequenting Rabit Hamil's house.

NED. Now, Mrs. Cary——

ELLEN. Ned, why don't you call me " Ellen ", as you used to?

NED. For a very simple reason. After Luke grew up I didn't think 'twas right.

ELLEN. I wish he'd never grown up!

NED. Well, Ellen — I may call you that again, for I've a notion I won't be long here — 'twas like this: I knew Luke and Sally were capering a bit, like a pair of kittens, but I hated to run to you with a bag of tales. And what's more: if you'd interfered at the wrong time, ten to one he'd have married her.

ELLEN. Sally Hamil's no kitten.

NED. No, I think Sally could kill a mouse all right. But I like Sally. She's bright and sharp and fearlessly honest. And she's got more gumption than Luke.

ELLEN. Well, they have him in the trap now, and they won't let him out easy. They'll skin him like an eel.

NED. I know it's bad. But 'twasn't my place to spy on Luke. I liked the boy and taught him to work: sure I carried him about the fields on my back. And he'd more sense then than he has yet.

ELLEN. His generation's all mad!

NED. Ah, don't say that, Ellen! I never lose my faith in youth. . . . Look at that young bay horse before I put him in the plough. It used to frighten me to watch him. Round and round the paddock, head and tail up, and kicking the shoes off his feet. . . . And where'd you see a sweeter horse in harness than he is to-day? You could rein him on a silk thread.

ELLEN. And you think it might be so with Luke?

NED. I do surely — just if he doesn't make a mess in the training.

ELLEN. What sort of a mess, Ned?

NED. There's only one sort of mess in this world. Luke's at every dance for ten miles round — or what they call a dance.

ELLEN. And he's learning to drink.

NED. He doesn't take much. . . . But a small quantity of poteen and a jazz band and a wild-eyed flapper make a risky cargo.

ELLEN. God knows it does!

NED. I wouldn't like to insure it against fire.

ELLEN. The very thought of it makes me shudder.

NED. Well, Luke's no longer a kid. If he makes a bad spill it's the first thing'll settle him. . . . It's a new age, Ellen. A new world. And you can't put your boy in a glass case.

ELLEN. I wish he'd marry a good sensible girl and settle down.

NED. Ay, a " good, sensible one ". I wonder now where he'd go to find her.

ELLEN. Oh, God only knows!

NED. Well, am I to go home, or stay here? Or go home and come back? Or what am I to do?

It goes to my heart not to finish the hay.

ELLEN. Isn't it cruel! If Peter wasn't coming, you and I'd go and finish it ourselves.

MAG *comes in.*

MAG. Mrs. Cary, if it's convenient I'll take my money now. I'm going for my shoes, and then to the dressmaker's.

ELLEN. All right, Mag, I'll get your money. . . . Ned, don't go away for a minute. [*She goes, left.*]

NED. Did you milk the cows?

MAG. Not damned likely. Let her milk them herself.

NED. Are you quitting us to-night?

MAG. Isn't it time to go when you're fired? I suppose if you were fired you'd go too?

NED. It's possible.

MAG. But you're not likely to lose your job.

NED. Nor you yours if you'd attended to it.

MAG. The widow Cary knows when she'd a big cod-fish on a string. Doing six men's work for half wages!

NED. I'm satisfied.

MAG. Some men are easily satisfied. A bit of empty flattery or a smile'd satisfy them.

NED. 'Twould take a great quantity of your smiles to satisfy a man.

MAG. 'Twill be different, though, when young Luke gets into the saddle. Your twenty years' brute-work may go here for sweet damn all.

NED. You haven't lost your time in Hamil's cottage. You're talking now like Rabit himself.

MAG. I'm talking like the whole parish. Aren't you the joke of nine square miles? Working day and night for a woman that wouldn't clean her boots on you.

NED. It strikes me you're not getting out of here a minute too soon.

MAG. I'm maybe not going far hence. I may still be able to watch how the cat jumps over here. I've a notion yourself and Luke won't die in double harness.

NED. I know where you're going. . . . You were cut out by Nature for Rabit Hamil.

MAG. Ned Shay, what are you after saying! Say that again, and I'll lift something and brain you!

NED. Ah, go to blazes. A decent polecat wouldn't pair off with that ould reptile.

MAG. As sure as heaven, I'll tell Rabit Hamil your words, and he'll stick a knife in you a foot long!

NED. Ah, go to blazes. The thought of it gives me nausea. You must have originally come out of a rabbit-hole.

ELLEN *comes in with money.*

ELLEN. You've ten pounds there, Mag. Count it.

MAG. Oh, I'm sure it's all right. There isn't enough of it to hold a mistake. Did you keep nothing off me for the three days I'll not be here?

ELLEN. No, I'm giving you that extra to get rid of you.

MAG. My God, aren't you pat! It's a wonder Ned Shay doesn't add to the bonus, for he's as scared of gossip as yourself. The pair of you should hire a deaf and dumb mute from the County Home. . . .

ELLEN. Now, Mag, you're just blue-moulding for a fight. But I'm not. I've a lot of things to do. I suppose you didn't milk the cows?

MAG. No, I left that for Ned Shay. 'Twill give him an excuse for hanging about the house till bed-time. [*She goes, right.*]

ELLEN. That's a good riddance, Ned. That lady has a bad streak in her.

NED. She's going to introduce a worse streak — crossing with Rabit Hamil.

ELLEN. Oh, Ned, Ned Shay!

NED. That explains a lot of other things. Rabit must get Sally off his hands at any price——

A motor-car is heard coming into the yard.

ELLEN. That's the car, Ned, with Uncle Peter.

NED [*goes to the door*]. 'Tis. Peter in his old Ford car, and well he's looking.

ELLEN. Don't go far away, Ned. You'll have a cup of tea with him. [*She gets busy about the fire.*]

NED [*shouts*]. Hullo, Uncle Peter!

PETER [*off*]. Hullo, Ned Shay! Are you never married yet?

NED. No . . . but 'twon't be soon now! [*He goes out.*]

ELLEN. 'Twon't be soon, indeed.

PETER *comes in. A vigorous little man, like a cattle-dealer in a modest way.*

PETER. Hullo, Ellen! Begor, you're getting younger and younger. . . . Will I kiss you?

ELLEN. If you like, Peter.

PETER. Begor, and I like. [*He kisses her. She gives a dry sob.*] Eh! what's wrong, Ellen? What's the matter, woman? I never seen the lip tremble before.

ELLEN. Something came over me. . . . I'm all right now.   Take a seat.

PETER. Here, Ellen: look me straight in the face. [*She does.*]   The health is good, anyhow.   You've an eye like a stag.

ELLEN. The health was never better, thank God.

PETER. But there's something else. . . . There's a wrong spirit in the air.   [*Looks round.*]   Where's the gossoon?

ELLEN. He's gone out.   He's got a motor-bicycle.

PETER. Is that he racing up and down the road trying to start it?   I thought I knew the legs of him.

ELLEN. That's Luke.

PETER. Got up like that?

ELLEN. Yes, got up like that.

PETER. A small farmer got up in a set of harness like that?

ELLEN. Yes, got up like that.

PETER. Where does he go with it?

ELLEN. I don't know.

PETER. You don't know.

ELLEN. No.   He goes out and never says where — and comes in when he likes.   He's doing badly, Peter — that's why I sent for you.   He's gambling on dogs, and going to dances, and selling my sheep unknown to me.

PETER. My God!   no wonder the heart gave a heave. . . .   After the fight you put up for him!

ELLEN. That's what hurts me.

PETER. Left with an infant in your arms, and a load of debt on your back — to sink or swim! . . . Ellen Cary, I could run out to the yard and raise a howl like a wolf!

ELLEN. Never mind, Peter.   I'm still young and

strong, and have a good bit of money. If you advise me, I'll buy another farm and start all over again.

PETER [*walks about*]. And that's my brother Luke's son! And, by heavens, he is Luke's son! No mistake about that. He never got that mental twist from his mother.

ELLEN. Now, Peter, let the dead lie!

PETER. I want to lay the blame on the right side of the house — my own side. That spectacle tearing along the road — with that leather outrage on its head — is hereditary. His father'd have gloried in it.

ELLEN. Peter, I wish you'd say no more.

PETER. Because you know I could say a lot more — and all to the same point. . . . But you're right, Ellen. You're right. Let the dead sleep. God save them all! [*He sits.*]

ELLEN [*gets a bottle*]. Does it do whiskey any harm to keep it a year in the house, Peter?

PETER. Begor, Ellen, I never was able to try the experiment.

ELLEN. But this was kept tightly corked.

PETER. Begor, mine wouldn't stay corked.

ELLEN. Will you taste this and see?

PETER. Ah, sure, that's fine stuff. But I'll have none of it — not till after I've seen Luke. My temper's bad enough, God knows.

ELLEN. I might have known better than offer it. [*She puts the bottle away.*] The tea'll be ready in a minute. Did Luke not know you passing?

PETER. If he did he never spoke. He was tearing up and down, trying to get the old thing started, and 'twouldn't give a kick.

ELLEN. For a very good reason — the plug of it is here on the dresser.

PETER. Good, begor! Let him heat his jacket along the road — let him tear away!

ELLEN. Now, Peter, you mustn't lose patience with him. He's not that old.

PETER. Ah, quit talking! A boy of seven should have more sense than that. When I was eighteen I was working twelve hours a day in a Glasgow foundry — making thirty shillings a week and sending a pound home. I knew every shop in Glasgow that sold stale bread and scraps of cheese.

ELLEN. Young people now are not the same.

PETER. I wouldn't want them to be the same. God forbid. But I'd want them to appreciate all the blessings they have that we hadn't.

ELLEN. They're that restless: and so many ways of taking them away from their work.

PETER. There was always plenty of ways of taking a fool away from his work. Does Luke work any at all?

ELLEN. Oh, he does. And Ned says when he's in the mood he's a fine worker.

PETER. Ay, in the mood! You'd think he was a poet. A young farmer must always be in the mood for work. A farm must be tickled and caressed like a child, or 'twon't smile.

ELLEN. Our farm's beautiful — thanks to Ned Shay. Every acre of it sparkling with health. And you know what it was twenty years ago — a wilderness.

PETER. Ellen, I'm going to ask you a pointed question, and don't take offence. Did you never think of Ned Shay as a partner?

P

ELLEN. That's very blunt, Peter. But I know you mean well.

PETER. I mean more than well — I mean business. I'm turning a plan over in my own mind — that's why I put the question.

ELLEN. Well, I did, Peter. Before Luke grew up I often thought of it.

PETER. Did Ned never make a move at all?

ELLEN. I never gave Ned any encouragement.

PETER. You were a fool, Ellen. 'Twas your place to speak. If Ned Shay'd made a move and you repulsed him, he'd have had to leave the country.

ELLEN. Would you be surprised to know, Peter, that I wasn't a free agent?

PETER. Begor, I would, Ellen . . . be astonished.

ELLEN. Your brother Luke on his death-bed made me promise never to marry again. He said if I broke my word he'd come back and haunt me.

PETER. Well, begor, I'd have let him come! And come within six months. . . . Lord, wasn't that like him! wear crape a whole lifetime for a dead wastrel! Ellen Cary, you were a fool to give that outrageous promise, and a bigger one to keep it.

ELLEN. Well, I've kept it too long to break it now. 'Tisn't worth breaking now. . . . You'll never mention that, Peter.

PETER. You never told Ned Shay?

ELLEN. No, I was afraid to talk about it. . . . At one time the least jerk would have broken it.

PETER. Well, begor, 'twas a dear promise! twenty golden years!

ELLEN. I'll call Ned. [*She goes to the door.*] Ned! come in for a cup of tea.

PETER. How does Luke and Ned get on together?

It's a wonder Ned doesn't strangle him.

ELLEN. There's been no trouble so far, but I wouldn't like to take a long lease. . . .

NED *comes in.*   ELLEN *gives them tea.*

NED. There's been a bit of a rumpus down at the road with Luke and the Hamils. I heard them scolding.

ELLEN. I'll go and see.

NED. You needn't mind. It's all over.

PETER. I seen Rabit Hamil and a young girl on the road.

ELLEN. That's Rabit's daughter Sally. Luke's been courting her, and dropped her, and she's going to've law.

PETER. Tell me this: is the boy an imbecile? I think we ought to spend a guinea on a good doctor. Sure nobody in his right mind would go near the Rabit Hamils. Didn't I know the whole breed forty years ago? They'd the mind of a rabbit, and the instincts of a rabbit, and the morals of a rabbit.

NED. The Hamils are gentry compared with the other party up at the corn mills.

PETER. Isn't that my argument — that he's a freak? Don't I know the corn mills party? Haven't I a grass farm up beside them?

ELLEN. People called Henly.

PETER. The Mad Henlys! The father was in the asylum twice. The sons are horse dealers — highway robbers. And there's either four or five wee, crafty, black-eyed baggages of girls — like gypsies — with not as much clothes on them as'd make a pair of leggin's for a hummin'-bird; and it's one of them Luke has out with him every night on this ould seaplane of his. . . . I tell you the end-up there'll be stark calamity.

ELLEN. That's terrible.

PETER. He'd the Biddy one — a slip of a school-girl — out the other night till three in the morning, and the father's vowing bloody vengeance. You'll have Mad Henly down here to-night or to-morrow, and the Lord have mercy on Luke Cary!

RABIT *comes in, blazing with anger.*

RABIT. Ellen Cary, your son attacked my daughter on the public road, and threatened to brain her with a spanner!

ELLEN. Did he strike her, Rabit?

RABIT. He run the bicycle up agen her, and pushed her into the hedge.

ELLEN. Was Sally not interfering with him?

RABIT. Not even looking his way. She was coming back here with the love-letters when Luke assailed her . . . and took them from her by main force. . . . I'm going straight to the Sargint.

ELLEN. Don't go away, Rabit. This is Uncle Peter. I want you to speak to him.

RABIT. Peter Cary, I didn't know you at all — I'm that excited.

PETER [*rising*]. Begor, it's my old friend, Rabit Hamil. [*Shaking hands*] I'm glad to see you, Rabit.

RABIT. I'm obliged to you, Peter.

PETER. Ellen, this is my old playmate. I know Rabit Hamil since I was in petticoats. The dacentest man from Hell to Omagh.

ELLEN. He doesn't waste his fine qualities on me, anyhow.

PETER. Then the fault must be on your side. For Rabit Hamil couldn't be uncivil for a wager. Haven't you something in a bottle, Ellen? I want to treat my old crony.

ELLEN. Sit down and take your tea. I'll give Rabit something if he wants it.

PETER. Of course he wants it. [*Sits.*] A good glass for old time's sake. He and I run the mountain together without a shoe on our feet. . . . Them was the days, Rabit.

RABIT [*mollified*]. Ay, God be wi' the times, Peter. There was no trouble then in the world. . . . D'ye mind the day we killed the nut-brown badger?

PETER. I was recalling the feat the other night.

RABIT. The marks of its teeth are still in my thigh.

PETER. I've told the story east and west.

ELLEN [*gives him a drink*]. You and Peter talk like old friends. But I thought you and I, too, were old friends.

RABIT. And we were, Ellen. Good friends — till your son put up the placards and declared war on me.

ELLEN. I'm not taking Luke's part. He's just like your own Sally — too smart and all for himself. The poor parents have no rights at all.

RABIT. Ellen Cary, you've gone to the roots of it. The parents have no rights, no control, no say in anything.

PETER. Now you pair's talking like one man. I've four sons and three daughters, and if I open my mouth they all seven laugh at me. All I'm good for is paying for their education. Drink up, Rabit.

RABIT. Your good health, Peter. And yours, Ellen. And I've nothing agen honest Ned Shay.

[*He drinks.*] 'Twon't be my fault if this civil war isn't settled quickly.

PETER. You hear that, Ellen. I told you Rabit Hamil was a man of peace. The finest man from Hell to Omagh. . . . Let's hear the rights of it.

ELLEN. Have I ever done you an injury, Rabit?

RABIT. Never, Ellen. But many a good turn you done me. You were good to my dying wife.

ELLEN. I may say I nursed her in her last illness, and buried her at my own expense.

RABIT. You did, Ellen. Lord reward you.

ELLEN. And when your son stole from his employer, I went to Captain McKane and bailed him out.

RABIT. You did, Ellen. Lord reward you again.

ELLEN. And for over twenty years you've made your living on our mountain, and I never charged you a penny.

RABIT. True again, Ellen. The Lord reward you for all.

ELLEN. The Lord's reward costs you nothing. But how do *you* reward me? By seizing the first chance you get to ruin me!

RABIT. Ruin you? Me?

ELLEN. Yes, you. My son's young — and more than foolish; and you're old — and more than crafty: and you set a trap for him and baited it with Sally.

RABIT. Ellen Cary, them's hard words. I'd take them from nobody but you.

MAG *comes in. She is dressed for going out: short skirt, and cheap pink stockings.*

ELLEN [*points to* MAG]. There's the root of the

trouble, Rabit. You want Sally off your hands, at any price, to bring in this young woman.

MAG. Mrs. Cary, for why are you dragging me in to it? . . .

RABIT. Hold your tongue, Kehoe! You've been gabbing already——

MAG. I never said a word——

RABIT. Hold your tongue, I say! Stand and be silent! You're the cause of all this domestic warfare.

ELLEN. I don't mind you and Mag getting married, Rabit. I know you need a wife, and Mag's a good worker. But you could have married her without trying to wreck my home.

RABIT. Ellen Cary, you've hit me a felling blow. But I'm taking it off your hand. D'ye know why? Because you were good to them that's gone.

ELLEN. I'd be good again, Rabit. I'd help you and Mag to-morrow, if you needed me.

RABIT [to MAG]. D'ye hear that?

MAG. I do.

RABIT. Then step across and beg Ellen's pardon.

MAG. For what am I begging it?

RABIT. Because I'm after telling you to beg it. Step across, then.

ELLEN. Come on, Mag. I'll meet you halfway. [They meet.] I hope we'll always be good neighbours, Mag. Rabit and we have been old friends so long.

MAG. Mrs. Cary, I'm sorry if I'm in fault.

ELLEN. It's all right, Mag. I wish you and Rabit a bed of roses.

RABIT. If she meddles with my old neighbours, she'll get a bed of whins. [To MAG] You'll stay with Mrs. Cary for three more days.

ELLEN. No, no!   I can manage myself.

MAG [*pleading*]. Let me stay, Mrs. Cary — if you please.

ELLEN. Oh, well — you may stay.

MAG. I was going for my shoes, but I can go to-morrow.   I'll change my clothes now and milk the cows.   [*She goes, right, glad to get away.*]

RABIT. Don't breathe a word of this to Sally. Sally doesn't know I'm taking in a wife.   Keep it quiet, Ellen, and I'll do as much for you.

ELLEN. We won't say a word, Rabit.

RABIT. I'll make Sally liberate Luke from all promises.   Is that fair?

ELLEN. Fair enough — if Sally agrees to it.

RABIT. Leave Sally to me.   I always have a fly in my hat to suit Sally's current.

SALLY *comes in with letters in her hand.*

SALLY. Mrs. Cary, here's a few love-letters.   Luke tried to grab them, but I held on to them.

ELLEN. I hope he didn't hurt you, Sally.

SALLY. Not a bit, Mrs. Cary.   I gave back as much as I got.   I like fighting with men.   [*She presents a letter.*]

ELLEN. You needn't mind, Sally.   I see Luke's writing. . . . I think your father wants to speak to you.

SALLY. Well, Rabit, what is it?

RABIT. Ellen Cary, will you tell poor Sally what you're after telling me?   Give poor Sally her due, she never heard it before.   She was small when the mother died, and staying away with her granny.

SALLY. What new stunt is this — about " poor " Sally?

ELLEN. Tell her yourself, Rabit. I don't want to rake up the dead.

SALLY. Rabit, what are you up to? What are you raising the dead for? Have you used up all the living?

RABIT. I've made my peace with this family, Sally. Ellen Cary has stirred up old memories.

SALLY. You're not going to cry, are you?

RABIT. No. . . . I've seen too much trouble in my time to cry now. Come on home, Sally, and I'll open my mind to you.

SALLY. You can open your mind here. Don't these people know all you want to say?

RABIT. You know, Sally dear, we're under a great debt of gratitude to Mrs. Cary.

SALLY. I know nothing of the kind. How did the debt originate?

RABIT. She nursed your poor mother, Sally, and put the last dress on her.

SALLY [shrinking]. Is that true, Mrs. Cary?

ELLEN. I thought you knew, Sally. Your father might have told you.

SALLY. No, he never told me. Nor he wouldn't tell me now, only in some remote way it happens to suit his own purpose. [To RABIT] What's behind it, Rabit?

RABIT. Gratitude, Sally.

SALLY. Gratitude in Rabit Hamil! I'll believe that when I've examined everything else. [Gives letters to ELLEN.] You can burn them, Mrs. Cary, and I'll burn the rest of them. [She goes out quickly.]

RABIT [elated]. Eh! didn't I tell you I'd a fly in my hat for Sally's current! The tears are up in her eyes. [He hurries out.]

PETER. Begor, that's the worst man from Hell to Omagh. He's as crooked as a barrel of serpents. I was sorry for that wee lassie.

NED. He's terrified of Sally hearing about the new stepmother.

ELLEN. I don't care what happens — if we get Luke out of their clutches.

NED. Luke's out now if he stays out. Sally wouldn't speak to him again after that. . . .

MAG *comes in, in her old clothes.*

MAG [*subdued*]. Mrs. Cary, will you please come outside? I want to speak a word, if you please.

ELLEN. Surely, Mag. [*To* NED] Take more tea if you want it.

ELLEN *and* MAG *go out.*

PETER. This boy's going to leave the mother without a roof over her head.

NED. Sometimes it looks that way.

PETER. Well, I've a plan in my head. I'm going to doctor the will and give his mother a life interest in the farm.

NED. She won't let you. And, anyway, Rabit Hamil knows what's in the will.

PETER. How does Rabit Hamil know?

NED. How does he know everything? You might as well try to conceal a thing from God.

PETER. If I can't doctor the will, I'll do something worse. I'll meet Luke on the road, and let him bash into the Ford. Better to lame or kill him than let him run wild through the world in that fashion.

NED. Peter Cary, will you take my advice? I know Luke better than his own mother does.

PETER. Well, what?

NED. I advise you to get into your car and go home. You're not the man to settle anything with Luke. He's nasty and ignorant, and you're hot-tempered, and the pair of you are certain to clash.

PETER. Well, damn the fut I'll go home — till I see him and give him a bit of my mind!

NED. Right. You'll see how it'll end.

ELLEN *comes in.*

PETER. Ellen, has Luke seen his father's will?

ELLEN. Never. But he'll have to see it very soon. He's talking about going to a lawyer.

PETER. I want to see the will — now. [*Takes out his specs.*]

ELLEN. It's over in Captain McKane's safe. I was afraid to keep it in the house.

PETER. I must see the will. I'll run over in the car and get it. A few minutes'll do it.

ELLEN. I was set on going over to-morrow, but we can as easily go to-night.

PETER. Surely. We'll go now. Get a hat on your head.

ELLEN. I must wash my face. . . . Ned, will you stay here till I come back?

NED. I will, surely.

ELLEN. 'Twon't take me long to get ready. [*She goes, left.*]

PETER. Ned Shay, you're a prize idiot! As big an idiot, sir, as ever wore pants.

NED [*surprised*]. How, Peter?

PETER. An idiot, sir; you didn't get your arms round Ellen Cary before her cub of a son grew up.

NED. Oh, is that all? I thought 'twas something serious.

PETER. Nothing could be more serious than that. I call it criminal. . . . Is there any more tea in that tea-pot? . . . I call it criminal. You deserve to be shot.

NED [*gets tea-pot*]. I always thought 'twas criminal to put your arms round the mistress without her consent.

PETER. Nonsense, sir! Not in this case. You'd every chance in the wide world. Sure she couldn't get along here without you. . . .

NED. I wouldn't call that a chance — I'd call it a handicap.

PETER. If you were a cold-blooded coward, 'twas Ellen's place to encourage you, sir!

NED. And why didn't she? Very little'd have done it.

PETER. If I tell you why . . . if I let you into a secret, will you take it with you to your grave?

NED. If it concerns Mrs. Cary, you can take it with you to your own grave. Anything she wanted me to know she always told me. If there's something she hasn't told me, then she didn't want me to hear it.

PETER. Lord above, such a wooden man! Such a frosted turnip! It's no wonder you're just where you started. A fine woman going to loss before your eyes. . . . If you'd been with Eve in the Garden of Eden, you'd be there yet.

NED. And maybe just as well.

PETER. You've helped to spoil the gossoon. You should have taken an ash-plant and whaled the everlasting divil out of him. . . .

NED. You should have been the hired man here, Peter. You'd have done a lot of things.

PETER. That gossoon at the right time wanted a man's fist about his ears——

LUKE *wheels in the bike. He is angry, and obscured with sweat and dust.*

LUKE. Where's she?

PETER. Is that you, Luke?

LUKE. Ay, who did you think 'twas?

PETER. Begor, I didn't know who 'twas. I never seen a small farmer harnessed like that before.

LUKE. Sure, I'm making no comment on your harness? What the hell is it your business what I wear? Are you paying for it?

PETER. Are you?

LUKE. I'm not asking you to pay, anyhow.

PETER. I know who's paying for it — your mother, with the sweat of her brow! But you'll pay for it in time. That's sure and certain. For the good God never intended you to be your own master!

LUKE. It's a pity she wasn't in to hear you. She can preach some herself, but she couldn't clerk to you——

PETER *stands up and bares his teeth.*

PETER. Open your fool face to me again!

LUKE [*draws a spanner*]. I'll open my face — and close it — when I'm ready.

NED. Peter Cary, sit down. I told you what would happen.

PETER. Could any man look at that monument of insanity and keep his temper? I ask you that — could he?

NED. And, sure, fighting like a pair of tinkers won't mend it.

LUKE [*turns on* NED]. What are *you* sticking your tongue in for?   You're another boss here!

NED *sits up, stiff and silent.*

PETER. Never mind, Ned.   Never mind.   I'll quarrel none with him.   [*Sits down.*]

LUKE. Am I calling your old Ford that's sitting outside a monument of insanity?

PETER. That old car's part of my living.   I attend five markets every week in it.

LUKE. And this old bike's part of my hobby. When I work all day in the fields I go out for a run at night.   Is there any monumental insanity in that?   If there is, the whole country must be one big asylum.

PETER. It's time enough for you to've a hobby when you can afford it.   You can't afford it now. Your mother can't afford it.   And the farm can't afford it. — That's what I'm trying to get at.

LUKE. Any farm that can't afford a six-pound hobby should be left to the crows. — That's what I'm trying to get at.

PETER. If you'd any pride in the land you'd make your work a hobby.

LUKE. But I've none.   I take no pride in drudgery. All that poetry about the young Irishman's passion for the red soil is bunk.   If the damned thing can't afford a decent living without tearing our guts out day and night — then it's only slavery, and should be worked by Chinamen.

PETER. Your six-pound hobby'll cost you a bit more before the Rabit Hamils and the Mad Henlys have done with you.   You've as many women dotted over the country as Brigham Young. If that's your notion of a hobby — or if it's your notion of Irish freedom — then every man who fought and died for it was a fool and an enemy of his race.

LUKE. He was hard up for a cause that fought and died for this country. I'd as lief fight and die for Spike Island.

PETER. When you get the farm you shouldn't waste your time growing oats and potatoes — you should grow petrol and potheen, and motor-bicycles and leather helmets——

LUKE. And old men. It's an ideal country for growing old men. They can live on a diet of legends about Brian Boru and the Big Wind.

PETER. It's better than a diet of greyhounds and Black African dances.

LUKE. If 'twasn't that 'twould be something else. Everything in this country is a mortal sin. It's a mortal sin to keep a greyhound, or a motor-bike. It's a mortal sin to go to a dance, or smoke a cigarette. It's a mortal sin to speak to a girl after sunset. . . . I don't know how the population of this country was over eight millions — at the time it was so holy, and no motor-bikes.

PETER. There's a trifling sin you've forgotten.

LUKE. Is it to be young? I meant to include it. For the most deadly sin of all is not to have a long, white beard. [*Loudly*] Curse all it is but jealousy! Forty hates twenty-five. Sixty hates forty. And seventy hates everybody.

PETER. What I had in mind was stealing a widow woman's sheep. And keeping Biddy Henly out till three in the morning. But maybe them's some of the new virtues.

LUKE. She's been talking to you. It's neither the old bike nor the leather helmet is bothering her — and you too. It's because I'm come of age and want into my own.

PETER. You'll be a long time in it — if you get it.

LUKE. There's no "ifs" about it. I'll get it, all right. Then it's nobody's business how long I'm in it, or how short.

PETER. I'll talk no more to you. I might as well talk to a naked savage.

LUKE. If you come down here to lecture me, you've lost your journey. [*To* NED] Did you see anyone tampering with my machine?

NED. Aren't you after telling me not to put in my tongue?

LUKE. I'm asking a question now.

NED. And of course I'm bound to answer the young master. [*Rising*] I won't tell you what I think of you.

LUKE. I'm in a sweat what you think of me. I know now who the news-carrier is. . . . You left me at six o'clock to go home, and I come back and find you having tea with Uncle Peter.

NED. A news-carrier!

PETER. Hit him a welt, Ned! Knock the clown rotten with a box. Or take him out to the yard and not lave a whole rib in him. . . .

NED. Keep quiet, Peter. His mother's in the room. I don't know which of you pair has the least sense. . . . I wouldn't strike Luke at all. Not because I'm afraid of him or his spanner, for he knows I'm not; but because I carried him about the fields on my back.

LUKE. I didn't mean anything, Ned.

NED. He wants rid of me, Peter. He's ashamed to act the clown in my presence. . . . Well, the farm's in good shape now, and I can walk down the road.

LUKE. I tell you I didn't mean it! Can't you listen to what I say?

NED. No, I can't listen — nor I won't listen! After twenty hard, happy years — I'm through here.

LUKE. You're not going, Ned?

NED. Yes, I'm quit. You'll have no trouble getting a man to stop work at six o'clock. Get one of your own kidney and he'll stop at four.

LUKE. I can get more machinery and work the farm myself.

NED. If you can I'm too long here. Whatever you do, good luck to you. I taught you all I knew about farming.

LUKE. I picked up a few things for myself.

NED. You did. You picked up a good deal of cheek. And plenty of gas. But you never picked up the main thing — intelligence. And till you get that, you've nothing.

ELLEN *comes in. She is dressed for going out.*

ELLEN. Where are you going, Ned?

NED. Luke will tell you. [*He goes out.*]

PETER. Ned's quit.

ELLEN. I was afraid — I'd a feeling 'twould come soon. What happened?

PETER. Luke called him a news-carrier.

LUKE. I did nothing of the kind. Didn't I tell him I didn't mean it? He'll be back in the morning.

ELLEN. My God! Ned Shay back in the morning! That shows all you know about the man who helped to nurse you.

LUKE. Ah, holy, holy! I wish nobody'd ever helped to nurse me! [*In a dancing rage*] Sure I never asked anyone to help to nurse me! I seem to be under a compliment to the whole country for helping to nurse me. If I mention the name of a man or woman within ten miles — they helped to nurse me! I wish to God I could meet someone that hasn't helped to nurse me. . . .

ELLEN. If you've blown off all your steam — I'm going out.

LUKE. What did you do to my machine?

ELLEN. I did nothing to it.

LUKE. I say you did! You tampered with it when I was in the room. 'Twon't give a kick.

ELLEN. I hope it never gives a kick. . . . Come on, Peter.

LUKE. Where are you going?

PETER. She's coming with me.

LUKE. Where are you going, I say?

ELLEN. Do you always tell me where you're going?

LUKE. You always know I'm going out.

ELLEN. And you seem to know I'm going out.

LUKE. But you always know I'm coming back.

ELLEN. I never know how or when 'twill be . . . whether you'll walk in or be carried in.

PETER. Come on, Ellen. Give him no information.

LUKE [*screams*]. Where are you going? My God! are you going to drive me mad?

ELLEN. Do you care a pin where I go?

LUKE. I do — I do!

ELLEN. Well, I'm going over to Captain McKane's.

LUKE. What to do there? . . . Here, I know! Wait a minute. I'll get you the price of your five sheep.

ELLEN. You'd better look sharp.

LUKE. Wait. It's in the room. [*He goes.*]

ELLEN. He thought I was going to have him arrested.

PETER. I'm sorry I didn't kidnap you, and keep you away for a month.

ELLEN. Don't speak to me, Peter. My heart's sore about Ned Shay. Was he very angry?

PETER. No, hardly a ripple.

ELLEN. That's all the worse. He'll never come back.

LUKE *comes in with money*.

LUKE. There — ten pounds.

ELLEN. Will you promise to steal no more of my sheep?

LUKE. I will.

PETER. Good. Come on, Ellen.

LUKE. Where are you going — now?

ELLEN. I'm going over to Captain McKane's.

LUKE. What are you going for?

ELLEN. I'm going over for your father's will. It's in Captain McKane's safe. And I asked Ned Shay to stay here and keep house till I came back.

LUKE [*angrily*]. And why couldn't you say that at first? Standing there making a great mystery of nothing at all!

ELLEN. That's right. The old snarl in your mouth the moment you know I'm coming back. . . . Listen, Luke, you've driven Ned Shay out, and I may give you as short notice. Be here when I come back. I'll hand you your father's will, and maybe tell you my intentions.

She and PETER *go out.*

LUKE [*shouts after them*]. If I find out who tampered with this machine, I'll walk in to the barracks and have them arrested! [*He starts tinkering at the motor.*]

Curtain

ACT III

The same scene.
MAG *is beating an egg in a pint mug.*
RABIT *comes in.*

RABIT. Kehoe, do I make threats like soap-bubbles?

MAG. Lord, Rabit, you're as deep as the pit.

RABIT. I said I'd shift Ned Shay, and he's gone. I said I'd shatter this homestead, and the walls are crumbling. There's only one beam left, and I'm sawing at it.

MAG. Down with it, Rabit! Let the roof crash!

RABIT. But you were within an ace of putting your feet in my traps. What in the divil's name possessed you to give our secret away to Ellen Cary?

MAG. I never opened my lip, Rabit. True to Heaven. 'Twas Ned Shay — curses on him! — guessed how the land lay and told the mistress. . . . I've got my wages here — ten pounds — if you're not too angry to take it.

RABIT. How could I be angry and wild in love at the same time? . . . How much other sum have you in the post office?

MAG. Over thirty pounds — interest and all.

RABIT. I'd my heart set on fifty. I'd my mind fixed on a wife with fifty pounds.

MAG. Well, haven't I got over forty?

RABIT. I'll make shift with the forty. You'll withdraw your money from the post office and place it in my keeping.

MAG. To-morrow morning. And I'll give you this ten pounds in a minute. Sit down now. I'm making you an egg-nog. We've the house all to ourselves.

RABIT. Good. After I get the egg-nog, you and I'll sit close. [*He sits.*] There's whiskey there in a bottle if you want it.

MAG. Just sit and compose yourself, Rabit. Leave everything to me. I know what a man needs, and when he needs it. That's what a woman is for, though few of them realise their duty. . . . 'Tisn't one girl in fifty can beat an egg correct.

RABIT. Fifty! One in fifty thousand!

MAG. Where they all make the mistake is in adding the spoonful of spirits to it before they add the milk.

RABIT. That's what they all do — add the wrong things first. Yourself alone can compound it to please me.

MAG. Take them traps off your back, Rabit. Don't be sitting with big, heavy traps on your back — compromising your lung-power.

RABIT. I always wondered what was stifling me if I sat down to rest myself. 'Twas these traps. [*Lays them on the floor.*]

MAG. 'Twas of course the traps. Every ounce of weight on a man's back is burning up his fuel. The very watch in his fob is burning up his fuel and taxing his strength. [*She adds milk and stirs with great energy.*]

RABIT. Looking back on my life, and the way I've been neglected, it's a wonder I'm alive to-day. I told Mrs. Cary that Sally could make nine kinds of soup out of a rabbit, but I didn't say 'twas nine kinds of poison.

MAG. Now, I'll add the whiskey and be you ready to quaff it off. [*She adds whiskey and stirs*] Now, Rabit: quaff it off. Never draw breath till you've drained the mug.

RABIT [*drinks*]. Mag, my heart, you excelled yourself in that brew!

MAG. Was it tasty?

RABIT. Tasty? 'Twas opulent.

MAG. You'll get three of them in the day till I make a new man of you.

RABIT. Then the sooner I'm under your care the better. Sally's clearing out to-morrow.

MAG. To-morrow! where to?

RABIT. To the married sister in Scotland. Damn the hair I care if she goes to the West Indies.

MAG. Lord, Rabit, the coast is all but clear. Here's the money — ten pounds — you'll be needing ready cash.

RABIT [*takes money*]. 'Tisn't far ten pounds'll go in a stylish wedding. For I mean to spare no expense. I'll take you for a whole day in a motor-car, and we'll stay a night or two at the seaside.

MAG. Lord, Rabit, I hope we get a nice sunny day. We'll drive slow — that everyone can see us. Will the man have ribbons on the car?

RABIT. He will, of coorse. Heavens, if he charges a pound, I think he'll have ribbons. . . . Come on, now, and we'll sit close.

MAG. I don't like to, Rabit. . . . [*She backs away.*]

RABIT. Come on, I say. [*Rising.*] Don't be running away now, for I'm too full of egg-nog to run after you. . . .

SALLY *comes in.*

SALLY. What sort of antics is this?

RABIT. What are you talking about? I see no antics at all.

SALLY. What were you trapezing after Mag for?

RABIT. I was trapezin' after nobody. . . . [*Sits.*]

SALLY. Where's Luke?

MAG. He's down at the blacksmith shop with the machine. And herself and Uncle Peter are over at Captain McKane's.

SALLY. Was there a big man and a wee girl — strangers — here looking for Luke?

MAG. No, I seen nobody.

SALLY. Maybe you were too busy. [*To* RABIT] What are you doing here?

RABIT. I dropped in a minute to rest my limbs.

SALLY. And do you get egg-nog in every house you drop into?

RABIT. What are you talking about?

SALLY. Sure, there's the mug and spoon, and the rest of it's on your chin.

RABIT [*wiping his chin*]. I got no egg-nog at all. 'Twas Ellen made that egg-nog for Uncle Peter, for I seen him taking it.

SALLY. And look at Mag — with the new light in her eye, and the bit of colour in her cheek. Mag, I'm sorry for you.

MAG. Sorry? Is it because I'm leaving here, Sally?

SALLY. Oh — I see : you're keeping this love-affair dark. . . . Well, it's all right, Mag; I won't mention it to a soul. You're getting a fine, careful husband. I'll bet he has your bit of wages in his pocket already.

RABIT. Mag Kehoe, speak up and shame this clip of a girl!

MAG. I don't know what you mean, Sally. My wages are upstairs in a box.

SALLY. Your wages are downstairs in Rabit's pocket. Wasn't I standing outside when you gave them to him.

MAG. Shame on you, Sally Hamil! you were listening to us talking.

SALLY. I heard every word of it. I saw you making the egg-nog, and saw Rabit taking it. Then he wanted to sit close.

RABIT. There now! I'll stand no more of this backbiting and calumny. I've suffered your imperence too long.

SALLY. Well, your sufferings are at an end. You and Mag can arrange for the motor-car with the ribbons. To-morrow night my bed'll be empty. [*She goes out.*]

RABIT. How'd you like to live in the house with that lady? You might as well be living under a microscope.

MAG. Lord, Rabit, I thought I'd faint away! She heard every word of us.

RABIT. Both heard and seen. That's what the accursed pictures does for them — make childer as cute as the fox.

MAG. But she didn't take it too bad at all. I was prepared for worse.

SALLY *comes in again.*

SALLY. Here's Mad Henly and his daughter coming now. . . . You've brought these people down here, Rabit——

RABIT. Me!

SALLY. Yes, you! I saw you writing the letter
. . . and you'll be sorry for it. For the man Henly
was in the madhouse, and should be in it still. . . .
Don't tell him where Luke Cary is, or you'll see
bloodshed.

As SALLY *goes out, right,* HENLY *and* BIDDY *come in
at the back. He is a big, coarse man, armed with
a heavy cudgel.* BIDDY *is a little flapper, with a
frightened look, and well dressed.*

HENLY. I'm John Henly of the corn mills. I'm
looking for the spalpin Luke Cary.

RABIT. I'm afeerd, sir, you're at the wrong house.

HENLY. I come off that bus. I was directed to
this house. Who lives here?

RABIT. This is my house.

HENLY. And who are you?

RABIT. My name you want, is it?

HENLY. Is your name Cary?

RABIT. It is not, thank God. There isn't a drop
of Cary blood in my veins.

HENLY. Where does Luke Cary live?

RABIT. You mean Mrs. Cary, the widow woman?

HENLY. I mean no widow woman! What the
godam sort of an eel are you? If you don't answer
me I'll crack your skull with the stick! Hasn't Luke
Cary a farm round here?

RABIT. I never heard of it. There's a Mrs. Cary
has a farm, and she's got a servant boy in the name
of Ned Shay.

BIDDY. That's them, Daddy!

HENLY. Where does she live?

RABIT. About three miles down the road. Turn

to the right when you step out my gate, and keep on straight till you come to a bridge. Mrs. Cary's house is just over the bridge — on the left-hand side. . . . And mind the dog.

HENLY. D'ye know Rabit Hamil?

RABIT. I've heard of him.

HENLY. What sort of man is he?

RABIT. Very respectable, they say. He was going on for the Church, but his health failed.

HENLY. Where does he live?

RABIT. He and his daughter live aback of the mountain, about ten miles to it by road. The daughter's going to marry a son of that widow Cary we were speaking of, they say.

HENLY. Is that the fella with the motor-bicycle?

RABIT. No, the one I mean has a steam-roller.

HENLY. Come on, gerl! I'll steam-roll a few of them! [*He and* BIDDY *go out.*]

MAG. Lord, Rabit, that's a wild Indian! He'll tear Luke Cary limb from limb.

RABIT. This is very serious! Luke's in trouble with both feet. She's under age, and if the father doesn't murder him, he'll be sent to gaol. Lord, what's the world coming to, anyhow?

MAG. Terrible, Rabit! Terrible . . . 'twill be a sad reproach in the neighbourhood.

LUKE *wheels in the machine. He is greatly excited.*

LUKE. Rabit Hamil, what are you doing here?

RABIT. I was waiting to see your mother — on business.

LUKE. You're a flaming liar! You're waiting for nobody at all — ye ould swine ye! ye brought them Henlys down here. . . . [*He makes a blind rush at*

RABIT, *who runs out.*]   Roast ye — I'll murder ye!

MAG. 'Twasn't Rabit Hamil brought them people down here at all.

LUKE. Here — scurse ye! you're going too! [*He hustles her out.*]   If you come in here again — either of you — I'll swing for you!

SALLY *comes in.*

SALLY. What's wrong, Luke?

LUKE. What do you want here?   Are you another wants choking?   There's the door!

SALLY. Easy, Luke.   Let me speak first, then shout as loud as you like. . . . Biddy Henly and her father are down here looking for you.

LUKE. I know — I know!   I know who brought them here, too . . . 'twas you or your father.

SALLY. 'Twasn't me, Luke.   It may've been Rabit. . . . I made Ned Shay waylay them and take them over to his own cottage, till I'd come here and tell you.

LUKE. Oh, holy!   the Henlys have no business with me at all!

SALLY. Ah, talk sense.   Could you sit five minutes with a girl and not ask her to marry you?

LUKE. Biddy Henly's only a small handful of a schoolgirl, I tell you, not seventeen. . . .

SALLY. All the worse for you.   That's why her father's on the warpath.   You'd Biddy out on the bike the other night and kept her out till near two in the morning.

LUKE. But I couldn't get rid of her!   I wanted to've her home at ten o'clock, but she made me take her round the coast . . . and the machine broke down three times.

SALLY. You were seen petting her when the machine crocked.

LUKE. It's a lie! I was cursing her sowl, and she whining and crying.

SALLY. I'll bet you won't take her round the coast again. Her father has half murdered her, and he's going to slaughter you outright.

LUKE [*almost in tears*]. What does he want coming here at all? 'Twasn't my fault—'twas Biddy's own fault. I couldn't get rid of her unless I'd thrown her off the machine.

SALLY. Ah, for heaven's sake, be a sport, and don't let the wee flapper down like that! Tell her father 'twas all your fault. Tell him Biddy wanted to be home at ten o'clock, but 'twas a gorgeous night and you took her round the coast.

LUKE. But her father'd warned me . . . he'd warned me if I took her out again he'd — he'd——

SALLY. He'd what?

LUKE. He'd have my blood!

SALLY. Wasn't that enough, then? What took you back after that? Why didn't you keep away from the corn mills altogether?

LUKE. I was up there on other business — up seeing the greyhound pup. Biddy met me on the road, and I couldn't get rid of her. She bounced on behind me, and I couldn't get her off. . . . You might as well try to shake off a nest of bees.

SALLY. Well, you'd better slip across to Ned Shay's cottage and speak to them.

LUKE. No, I will not! I wouldn't face her father for a thousand pounds.

SALLY. Then he'll come over here, and you'll have to face him before your mother and Uncle Peter.

LUKE [*starts howling*]. I tell you I've done nothing wrong at all! But I'm afeerd of her father . . . a big, ugly rascal of a man with insanity in him.

SALLY. You never had to kick me off your machine.

LUKE [*drying his eyes*]. I wish I never'd got the damned thing at all. . . . I wish I was dead and buried. . . . There's Ned Shay gone from us, and my mother talking about going, too.

SALLY. And I'm going, too. You and I are quits. Rabit's bringing in a wife, and I'm fading out.

A motor is heard off.

LUKE [*jumps*]. I hear a car!

SALLY. Well, don't jump out of your harness. Your nerves are all in your mouth. It's only your mother and Uncle Peter.

LUKE. What'll I do, Sally?

SALLY. Stand your ground like a man. Now's the time to've it thrashed out — if Biddy has no claim on you.

LUKE. She's none, I tell you!

SALLY. Maybe she's a claim on somebody else, and you're going to be the goat. . . . I told you a hundred times to keep away from them wee flappers — as silly as yourself. . . . But you're such a championship idiot!

ELLEN *comes in.*

ELLEN. Ned Shay and the Henlys are coming here, and Uncle Peter doesn't want to meet them.

LUKE [*shaking*]. I'm going outa this!

SALLY [*stops him*]. Don't be a fool! This is serious. You can't afford to run away. . , .

LUKE. Let me go, Sally! Let me go, or I'll yell!

SALLY. Where are you going?

LUKE. I'll stay in the room. If the Henlys say I did anything wrong I'll come out and face them. . . . Let me go now, or I'll knock you down.

SALLY. All right, go to the room. I'll stay here and talk to the Henlys.

LUKE. Do, Sally — talk to them. I've told you all that happened. . . . I'm innocent. [*He flings off, right.*]

SALLY. And you look it!

ELLEN [*taking off her hat*]. Do you know these people, Sally?

SALLY. Not very well, Mrs. Cary. But the man Henly was in the madhouse, and Luke's afraid of him.

ELLEN. Thank God, Ned Shay's coming!

SALLY. This may be a lesson to Luke. 'Twill put him from running after wee flappers — as silly as himself. And you needn't worry about me, Mrs. Cary. Luke and I are quits.

NED *and* HENLY *and* BIDDY *come in.*

NED. Mrs. Cary, this is Mr. Henly and his daughter. They want to see Luke.

HENLY. This is his godam machine! Where's he?

ELLEN. He's about the house, I think.

HENLY. Get him!

ELLEN. Has my son done anything wrong, Mr. Henly?

HENLY. Get him! If he hadn't, would I be here? This is my daughter — a trifle over sixteen. Your spalpin took her out the other night and brought her back at three in the morning. D'ye call that anything wrong?

ELLEN. I do, indeed. I call it terribly wrong. Has Luke been frequenting your house?

HENLY. I caught him there once. I kicked him out to the road. I told him if ever he come back I'd murder him. I'm here now to keep my word. Get him!

NED. Mr. Henly, you're far too angry to get the right view of this affair. If Luke Cary has broken any law, you've a remedy. But you'll murder nobody in this house.

HENLY [*menacing* NED]. Who'll stop me? I say, who'll stop me! Would you stop me? What!

NED. Now, keep cool. You could be stopped. I'm not taking Luke's part. He's a foolish boy. But I've seen young girls — about the age of this one — pestering him for a run on the bike.

HENLY. I kicked him out once. I told him never to come back. Wasn't that enough?

NED. That ought to've done it. You're not like a man Luke'd care to offend twice. That's why I think this young girl maybe . . . [BIDDY *starts a whine*.] Now, don't cry, dear. I'm not blaming you at all.

HENLY. Here, where's the spalpin? It's him I come to see — not the sarvant man. Get the spalpin!

ELLEN. Will I call Luke, Ned?

SALLY. Half a minute, Mrs. Cary. I want to speak to Biddy. [*To* BIDDY] You ought to cough up, kid, and not have these big men killing one another.

BIDDY. Don't know you.

SALLY. But I know you, Biddy. You're legion. I wasn't far away the other night when you bounced on Luke Cary's machine without being asked.

BIDDY. Did not!

SALLY. You did so. Luke wasn't up there seeing you at all. He was on other business.

HENLY. Name it — the other business!

SALLY. He's got a greyhound pup on the grass — 'twas up seeing it he was. And this wee girl met him on the road and lit on him like a June bee.

HENLY [*grabs* BIDDY]. Is that true?

BIDDY. 'Tis not!

SALLY. Then let's hear your own way of it.

BIDDY. He met me near the mills.

SALLY. By appointment?

BIDDY. Don't know.

SALLY. But I know. He never'd a date on with you after your father gave him the boot. Had he now?

BIDDY. No — yes — no. I'm not sure. I think he had.

SALLY. Mr. Henly, I know what I'm talking about. Luke Cary never went back after you gave him the warning.

HENLY [*grabs* BIDDY]. Did he meet you on the road by chance or by tryst?

BIDDY. By — I think — chance.

HENLY. Did you lep on the machine without bein' bidden? If you did I'll pull the tripes outa ye!

SALLY. Lord, man! how do you expect the kid to tell the truth under a threat like that? Give her half a chance. Even if she did get on the machine, she knew the owner. . . . If you don't frighten her she'll tell the truth and never be naughty again. . . . Won't you, Biddy?

BIDDY. Will.

R

HENLY. Go on then — out with it!

SALLY. Here, let me talk to her. . . . Now, Biddy, your father's a nice big man, and he's quite right to keep you off the tail-end of motor-bikes. That's no place for you at all. You might as well be sitting on a coffin-lid. But he'll forgive you this time if you tell the truth. Now, split fair, Biddy: wasn't it your own fault?

BIDDY. Was. . . . I got on myself.

SALLY. Didn't Luke want to fetch you home at ten o'clock.

BIDDY. Did.

SALLY. But 'twas a gorgeous night, and you made him take you round the coast?

BIDDY. Did.

SALLY. And the machine crocked two or three times?

BIDDY. Twice.

SALLY. And Luke cursed like a dragoon?

BIDDY. Did.

SALLY. Now, Biddy, one other question. And, mind, I've been out with Luke Cary — scores of times — at every hour of the day and night. Did he ever attempt to kiss you in his life?

BIDDY [*quickly*]. No! No!

SALLY. I know, Biddy. He's a mutt. I've been disappointed myself.

HENLY. Are you sure about that?

BIDDY. I am — I am. He was always talking about speed motors.

HENLY. You're sure now?

BIDDY. I am! He's a fool. . . . 'Twas only to laugh at him I went out.

SALLY. You see, Mr. Henly: Biddy knows her

way about. She knows who to go out with — don't you, Biddy?

BIDDY. I do — I do! There's boys I wouldn't go out with at all.

HENLY [*to* ELLEN]. Get him! I want to renew the caution before witness. After that, let him beware. I'll kill him like a rat.

SALLY. Go on, Mrs. Cary: call Luke.

ELLEN [*at room door*]. Luke, come here a moment. Mr. Henly wants to caution you again.

LUKE *comes in.* BIDDY *looks at him sidewise and grins.*

HENLY [*grabs hold of* LUKE's *lapels*]. D'ye know me, sir?

LUKE. I do.

HENLY. Ever seen me before?

LUKE. I have.

HENLY. Did I kick you out of my yard?

LUKE. You pushed me out.

HENLY. I kicked you out — like a dog! Did I, sir?

LUKE. Well, we won't argue.

HENLY. I told you never to come back!

LUKE. And I didn't.

HENLY. Hadn't you my child out again on your godam machine?

LUKE. I couldn't keep her off it.

HENLY. By the 'tarnal Moses! if I ever catch you again within three mile of my house — I'll kill you first, and then drown you in the mill-dam! D'ye hear me, sir?

LUKE. I DO.

HENLY. The country's lousy with the likes of you!

Roast the brain that invented these atrocities! A farmer can't walk the road he's paying for! He can't drive his cows to the field, for fear of some leather-coated hyena like you tearing up and laming them on him. . . .

ELLEN. It's the honest truth, Mr. Henly. I'm afeerd to drive our own cows across the road.

HENLY [*shaking him*]. If you were my son d'ye know what I'd do with you? I'd chain you at the turf-stack for six months, and throw you a crust of bread like a dog. If that didn't cure you, I'd put you in a bag and drown you!

ELLEN. Luke had no father, Mr. Henly.

HENLY. None of them seems to've any father nowadays! [*Shakes him.*] But there's still an odd man left that can handle the boot and the fist. [*He shoots* LUKE *off, and aims a kick at him.*] Beware of me, sir!

LUKE. Ah, gotta hell, ye madman ye! And keep your daughters in off the road. Sure every fella in the county's afeerd to pass the house. . . . They come out and light on him like a flock of crows! [*He tears off to the room.*]

HENLY [*spits on the stick*]. I'll go and varnish this stick with his blood!

SALLY. Now, Mr. Henly, you've varnished him well enough. . . . Your daughter's come to no harm — that's the main thing. And your bus goes past the gate in two minutes.

HENLY [*grabs* BIDDY]. Come on, you! I'll put you from leppin' up behind spalpins. [*He drags* BIDDY *out.*]

ELLEN. Thank God to see the heels of that man! Only for you, Sally, we were wrecked and ruined.

PETER *comes in.*

PETER. You're lucky people. I never knew Mad Henly to come out for scalps and go back without them. I never knew him to leave a whole head in a house before. Is Luke rid of him?

ELLEN. He is — by a miracle. That's the only sort of man Luke seems to understand.

PETER. Well, have you told Ned Shay what I suggested? — I haven't long to be here.

ELLEN. I haven't got speaking to Ned yet.

LUKE *comes in. He's taken off part of the harness.*

LUKE. Ned Shay, aren't you coming back to work?

NED. No. . . . I only came over to keep that madman from wrecking the house.

LUKE. You're coming back, Ned. I'm out of trouble now, and I'll keep out of it.

NED. The same here. I can work anywhere.

ELLEN. Luke, you're only insulting Ned. I told you he wouldn't come back.

LUKE. If Ned isn't here, I'll not be here!

ELLEN. Why not?

LUKE. Because you'd always be chewing the rag about him helping to nurse me, and I'll have none of it! That's why.

ELLEN [*gives him document*]. There's your father's will. In a few more days you'll own everything here. Then if I chew the rag you can show me the door.

PETER. That's the style, Ellen. You're not depending on him. You've me at your back.

SALLY. If you're going to wind up your family affairs, I'll get. So long, Luke.

ELLEN. Luke, if you're a son of mine you'll give

Sally a good present. She got you out of that Henly affair with a whole crown.

SALLY. Thanks, Mrs. Cary; I don't want a present. My father wanted money, but I wanted Luke. Now I want neither Luke nor his money. [*She is going.*]

LUKE. Sally: where are you going?

SALLY. I'm going over home. There's a good programme on from Daventry.

LUKE. When are you going away?

SALLY. To-morrow.

LUKE. Where are you going?

SALLY. To my sister in Scotland.

LUKE. What to do there?

SALLY. To learn to be a nurse — if I can raise the wind. . . . Wait till you see me over here next summer — in a blue uniform, and a poke bonnet with fliers.

LUKE. Sally, come here a minute. . . . Will you take me on again?

SALLY. What's the big idea?

LUKE. I'll go with you to Scotland.

SALLY. No, indeed, you won't. Nurses don't marry young. At forty or fifty they adopt an old patient with plenty of dough and kill him off in three months.

LUKE [*impulsively*]. I'm going with you — I don't care a damn! [*He tears up the will.*]

ELLEN. Luke, you're destroying the will!

PETER. Quiet, Ellen! let him tear it and eat it!

LUKE [*scatters the fragments about*]. There! I make you a present of the property. You'll never be able to say that I put Ned Shay out of a job, or you out of a home.

PETER. He's mad! The head's away.

LUKE. Maybe I'm mad! Or maybe yourselves are mad. I think I know what I'm doing — I'm smashing the leading-strings. I'll go now where I like, and do what I like. I won't be herded and watched and lectured morning, noon, and night, by a lot of old sticks! . . . Come on, Sally. I've smashed the tether. I'm as free now as yourself.

SALLY. Where do you think you're going?

LUKE. I don't know yet. I'm going somewhere, anywhere. If there's a place on earth where the people didn't help to nurse me — I'll go there. Come on, Sally; I'll walk the road with you.

SALLY. No, you won't.

LUKE. You don't want me? Mind, I'm not going down on my knees.

SALLY. 'Twouldn't matter to me if you did. I don't want you, and I'll tell you why. Your mother once did mine a good turn, and then opened the grave and took her out of it.

ELLEN. I never meant to hurt you, Sally. I only wanted to shame your father.

SALLY. It's all right, Mrs. Cary. I've let Luke out of the trap.

LUKE. I don't want out of the trap!

SALLY. Your mother helped a brother of mine, too, when he stole something from somebody.— That's another bit of family history I've only come into.

LUKE. That's got nothing to do with you at all. I've stolen sheep myself, and money too. I'd to steal eggs and sell them to get cigarettes and petrol. She only give me sixpence on Saturday night, and a shilling at Christmas. Isn't that meaner than stealing? . . .

ELLEN. Sally, let him walk over home with you.
'Twill settle his nerves. If you can agree on any
plan, come back and tell me. It's my opinion you're
far too good for him.

LUKE. Come on, Sally. If she'd said that at first
she'd have saved the riots.

SALLY. I'll not walk down the open road with
you.

LUKE. Well, we can go down by the meadow.
. . . Come on, Sally; we'll go and finish the hay.

He and SALLY *go out.*

PETER. Now, Ellen, you have him at your mercy.
There's the will — in flitters. You have him at
your mercy.

ELLEN. What's the use in having your own child
at your mercy? We can maybe patch up the will.

PETER. Can we, indeed! [*He collects several pieces
and burns them.*] You won't patch it up now!
You'll give him a few pounds and be rid of him.
Take him on the jump, and he'll give you a clear
receipt. . . . What do you say, Ned?

NED. I don't like it, Peter. We want the boy
rooted in his father's farm, not rooted out of it.

ELLEN. Ned's right, Peter. What use is an oldish
woman on the land? Isn't she only a piece of
lumber? A farm without children growing on it
might as well be under the sea.

PETER. And will you let him bring Rabit Hamil's
dandy doll in here. . . . Will you stay here and
wash dishes for them?

ELLEN. If Sally suits him, she'll suit me. Luke
isn't such a catch in himself.

PETER. Well, by gor! It's no use trying to settle

anything for a woman. As quick as you make a plan she fires off a torpedo. . . .

ELLEN. I'll go and bring Luke and Sally back, and we'll reason it out with them.

PETER. You're a fool, I tell you! Let him go a year to Scotland — 'twill make a man of him.

ELLEN. 'Twould more likely make him a corner boy. Then he'd come back to me and bring a dirty wife and child with him.

PETER. And will you stay here as slavey? Because if you do, Ellen, I wouldn't come to your wake.

ELLEN. You shouldn't be too hard on him, Peter, for there's a big streak of yourself in him.

PETER. Run after him, then, and beg his pardon. And bring him back for Ned Shay to beg his pardon. Then I'll beg his pardon and go home.

ELLEN. Stay here, Ned, till I come back. [*She goes.*]

PETER. It's no wonder the young people are autocrats, for the ould people are slaves! By heavens, I'll not let my family walk over me in that fashion! I've four sons and three daughters, and as they come of age I'll lead them out to the gate and give each of them a good fat kick, and say — " That's your fortune. Go and invest it and live on the interest."

NED. I advised you, Peter, to go home, but you wouldn't heed me. You clashed with Luke, and got me out of a job. . . . I think you ought to slip away home now.

PETER. This country's going to hell at a hundred mile an hour! Petrol and pictures and potheen and jazz and doles and buses and bare legs and all sorts of foreign rascalities. You and I were content to toil and moil for a living, but the new breed wants to be well paid, well fed, and idle.

NED. I must be short-sighted, Peter, for I see nothing wrong. The changes I see are all for the better. I like to see the big bus stopping at the end of the road to lift the kids for school. . . . Lord, it must be great to be a kid and go to school on a bus!

PETER. It's a wonder you and Luke couldn't get on well together — for you're as big a fool as himself!

NED. 'Twasn't my fault, Peter. I always tried to see the boy's point of view. D'ye see that motor-bike? That's the evolution of the low-backed car. The boy that rides on that isn't the one that sat beside " sweet Peggy ". . . . He's a new gossoon altogether, and demands new treatment.

RABIT *and* MAG *come in, scolding.*

RABIT. I'm rid of you now! Go your ways. I want no more ado with you. 'Twas you and your evil gossip made the havoc on this quiet home-stead.

MAG. Gimme back my money, then! Back with it — ye stinking ould trapper ye! Ned Shay was right — a decent polecat wouldn't be in the same field with you!

RABIT. You gave me no money, hussy!

MAG. Infernal liar! I gave you my ten pounds and you have it in your inside pocket. . . .

RABIT. Where is Ellen Cary? — Till I tell her the stories this evil-tongued Kehoe has broadcast in the parish.

MAG. I'll see Mrs. Cary myself when I come back. [*She hurries out, right.*]

RABIT. I say, friends, we're well rid of that blade.

If she'd been here another month she'd have ruined every character in the parish.

NED. She might have ruined yours, too, Rabit.

RABIT. She couldn't injure yours or mine, Ned. Your character's beyond reproach, and mine's beyond repair. . . . But that's not my story. Luke and Sally have made it up again. They've gone down by the meadow to mingle their tears together. And now, Shay, it's your move.

NED. What do you mean?

RABIT. If I get Sally planted in here——

NED. " If! " She isn't in yet.

RABIT. She's very near it. And if you've as many brains as a dog-daisy you'll put no obstacle in the way. For if Sally walks in here, Ellen Cary walks out. And she doesn't walk out a pauper: she's hard money enough to buy another farm.

PETER. The ablest man from Hell to Omagh! That's my own plan, Rabit. Ellen to buy a farm, and Ned Shay to go and work it.

RABIT. Work it? If that's all Ned Shay can do, he deserves to sew on his own buttons for ever. . . .

ELLEN, LUKE, *and* SALLY *come in.*

ELLEN. I've lost my journey. Luke and Sally can settle nothing at all.

RABIT. Whose fault is it? If it's Sally's, I'll soon make her surrender. I've sent Mag Kehoe packing, and upset all my domestic arrangements.

SALLY. Is that right, Rabit? Have you broken with Mag?

RABIT. What do you take your father for? Would I wed with a menial, and you going to be a farmer's wife? D'ye think I've no family pride in me at all?

SALLY. Luke doesn't want to be a farmer. He's destroyed the will.

RABIT. Eh! when did this happen? I was afeerd of this. . . . This is some of Ned Shay's work, or Uncle Peter's.

LUKE. 'Twas my own work. I don't want the farm at all.

RABIT. What then do you want a wife for? Are you going to marry and live on a motor-bicycle? . . . Sally, mind what you're doing. Luke Cary without a farm is no match for anyone. I've caught better husbands in a rabbit-trap.

SALLY. Luke and I are not coming in here to put his mother out — that's final.

LUKE. If she gives me fifty pounds, I'll sign a paper and clear out.

ELLEN. I'll give you no money. I'll give you your father's farm, and make your best of it. And don't fret about me. I can look after myself.

RABIT. Here's a plan, Ellen. Captain McKane has three farms for sale — forty, fifty, and eighty acres. Buy the middle one, Ellen, and take Ned Shay with you to manage it. Ned, as you know, is a quiet, sober, innocent, God-fearing young man.

PETER. Begor, Rabit, it's a first-rate plan. I'm all for that.

RABIT. There's a fine red-brick house on the fifty-acre farm ; the Captain built it for the land steward. . . .

PETER. Ned Shay, come outside a minute. I want to tell you a secret. [*He and* NED *go out.*]

RABIT [*looking after them*]. I wonder now what them pair of grass-fed meddlers are after! I've got my ducks all in a row if they leave me alone. . . .

MAG *comes in, right, dressed and carrying a portmanteau.*

MAG. Rabit Hamil, I'm for the road. Gimme my ten pounds!

RABIT. Wait a minute. First tell Mrs. Cary the slander stories you've been circulating about herself and Ned Shay.

MAG. It's a lie, Mrs. Cary! 'Twas Rabit himself put the slander in my ear. He told me yourself and Ned Shay were secretly married, seven years ago, and you'd three childer in a orphanage.

ELLEN. Oh, saints above — such wickedness! Three children in an orphanage!

RABIT. Could you believe it, Ellen? Could you believe that Mag Kehoe — and she aitin' your bread — 'ud give feet to such a vile story?

MAG. How could I give feet to a seven-year-old story and I only here a twel-month?

SALLY. Here, Rabit: give Mag her bit of money and let her go.

RABIT. Come outside, then. I'll pay you off and show you the broad road. You thought you'd me in a Ford car with ribbons flying in the breeze. But I'd the ribbons up once, and that was enough for me. My aim is to erect a hut on the summit of the mountain, where I'll never see one of your sex.

MAG. That you may die in it — polecat! or be burnt to a cinder in it!

RABIT. Either is preferable to living with you in it. . . . Step along now, and be silent.

He and MAG *go out.*

ELLEN. Luke, did you ever hear that frightful gossip?

LUKE. No, nor nobody else.

SALLY. Rabit coined that story to frighten Mag. He thought she'd run away without her money.

LUKE. Look here, mother. There's far too many people meddling in our affairs. Let's settle it ourselves. Buy me one of McKane's farms, and you and Ned Shay can stay here. Isn't that simple enough?

SALLY. That's the solution now, Mrs. Cary. You won't have to leave your home. . . .

ELLEN. But the people might say I swindled you out of your father's farm.

LUKE. Ah, roast the people! Sure, if you go they'll say I put you out of your home — and that's worse.

ELLEN. Well, I think, in God's name, we'll settle it in that way. I'll buy you the farm with the house on it, and stock it for you. I was going to buy it for myself. . . . I hope I'm doing the right thing.

LUKE. Right or wrong, I'm content.

SALLY. And me too. I'll have the nicest house in Ireland.

ELLEN. I hope you will, Sally. . . . And if you've any childer, don't expect too much off them, then you won't be disappointed. [*She goes off, left.*]

SALLY. She's gone now to've a good cry to herself.

LUKE. What's she got to cry about?

SALLY. Don't be a barbarian! . . . I'll teach you how to treat your mother.

LUKE. Surely, Sally. Surely, I'll treat her any way you like. . . . Here, gimme a kiss for luck.

SALLY. I'll give you no kiss. I'm not marrying you to sit and kiss me. You're going to work.

LUKE. Good Lord! have I only broken one tether to be tied with another?

SALLY. That's all. Only a change of caretakers.

LUKE. Well, I've something to work for, anyhow. I'd rather have you, Sally, than all in the world.

SALLY. I'll kiss you over at the new house. . . . Go and get into your harness; we'll run over and inspect the place.

LUKE. Right, Sally. Uncle Peter could run us over in the car.

SALLY. Don't be a thick! We can go ourselves. . . . I'll fix up this machine; I know what it wants.

LUKE. And will you sit on it, Sally?

SALLY. You bet! A motor-bike's all right and very useful — if the owner's all right.

LUKE. I declare to Heaven, Sally, she's a powerful engine altogether! You'd hear the rips of her like a flying-machine. . . . I'll go and get into the togs. [*He goes, left.*]

SALLY *puts in the plug,* ELLEN *comes in.*

SALLY. Luke and I are going over to inspect the farm.

ELLEN. That's all right, Sally. I don't mind now where he goes — when you're with him.

SALLY. I'll kiss you for that. [*And she does.*] You needn't have another moment's anxiety about Luke. I could tie him round my umbrella. He'll come to Ned Shay for any advice he wants, about cattle and things, and I'll come to you.

ELLEN. Sally, dear, I believe you'll make him a good wife. I thought you'd be very flighty.

SALLY. Ah, that's what they all think — that we young people are mad. But I'm getting the makings of a good husband, and a good home — and I'll watch both. . . . And now it's your turn to be happy. You're going to marry Ned Shay.

ELLEN. Sally, dear, be careful! Don't say a word. You know we're very old-fashioned people.

SALLY. Ah, my eye! the fashion never changes — it's only the frills change. . . . I'll make the match in two ticks.

NED *and* PETER *come in.*

We've settled everything ourselves, as women have to do in the end. Luke and I are going to the new farm, and these two Michaelmas daisies are staying here.

PETER. Begor, it's a first-class settlement.

SALLY. Now, Ned, it's up to you. You've been in love with Ellen Cary for twenty years, and she in love with you.

NED. Who told you, Sally?

SALLY. The birds. Is any young man going to work day and night for half wages unless he's in love with somebody?

NED. Couldn't he be in love with his work?

SALLY. Ah, my boot! That might suit a pale artist. But no healthy man falls in love with hard work unless there's a woman in it. You've had a glorious time, Ned. If you didn't know before what sweetened your daily toil, you know now. You pair were actually married, man. A sort of spiritual-cum-agricultural union between a fine man and a finer woman.

PETER. Begor, Sally, I'm your Uncle Peter. And proud of it! In that wee cropped head of yours is the wisdom of the ages.

SALLY. I'll go and tell Luke he's got a stepfather . . . he's been an orphan long enough. [*She goes, right.*]

PETER. Before I go home, Ellen — is all settled? I've told Ned about that outrageous promise.

ELLEN. Say no more, Peter. I never want Luke or Sally to hear it. And don't tell your wife.

PETER. It's buried, Ellen. [*To* NED] Take her, Ned. You deserve her, and that's saying a whole lot! Good fortune to you both. I'll come and dance at your wedding. [*He goes.*]

NED. Ellen, are we dreaming?

ELLEN. I think we must be, Ned.

NED. You must have been a strong-minded woman.

ELLEN. I was anything but that. I was a born coward. I've wanted this to happen every day for fifteen years.

NED. And I for twenty. . . . Well, it's happened now. And in a curious way. . . . In the long run, Ellen, it always pays to keep the straight road. [*He kisses her.*] Will you believe it, I've grown young again in a moment.

ELLEN. And I, too, I'm ashamed of how young I feel——

RABIT *in the doorway.*

RABIT. Ned Shay, what about them placards? I suppose now you own the mountain and all?

NED. Tear them down, Rabit. And get the hut on the summit as soon as you like.

ELLEN. Long may you enjoy the privilege, Rabit.

RABIT. Thank ya, Ellen. And you, Ned. And may fortune make you both her favourites. . . .

The mountain is my ould sweetheart. I'll live and die on it, and be buried on it. And, if it's possible, I'll come back and poach on it for all eternity. [*He goes.*]

> LUKE *and* SALLY *come in.* SALLY *is wearing the helmet.*

SALLY. Well, is all okay?

ELLEN. Oh, I think so, Sally. Uncle Peter settled everything.

LUKE [*wheeling out*]. Come on, Sally.

SALLY. Luke's a bit shy about the new stepfather, but he doesn't mind. He'll soon get used to Father Ned.

LUKE. I'm not a bit shy. Good luck to them. It's their funeral. [*He wheels out.*]

SALLY. Now, Ned, don't be a mutt. Buckle in and make up for lost time. You've a lot of leeway to make up. . . . [*Grinning.*] You pair ought to go and finish the hay. [*She goes.*]

ELLEN. It might be a very good plan, Ned.

NED. What, Ellen?

ELLEN. To go down to the meadow and finish the hay.

NED. But I know a better plan. [*He shuts the door, sits down beside her.*] It's right here we'll finish the hay. [*He puts his arms round her.*]

THE END

Printed in Great Britain by R. & R. CLARK, LIMITED, *Edinburgh.*